30 LESSONS FOR LIVING

30 LESSONS FOR LIVING

Tried and True Advice
from the
Wisest Americans

KARL PILLEMER, PH.D.

HUDSON
STREET
PRESS

HUDSON STREET PRESS
Published by the Penguin Group
Penguin Group (USA) Inc., 375 Hudson Street, New York, New York 10014, U.S.A.
Penguin Group (Canada), 90 Eglinton Avenue East, Suite 700, Toronto,
Ontario, Canada M4P 2Y3 (a division of Pearson Penguin Canada Inc.)
Penguin Books Ltd., 80 Strand, London WC2R 0RL, England
Penguin Ireland, 25 St. Stephen's Green, Dublin 2, Ireland (a division of Penguin Books Ltd.)
Penguin Group (Australia), 250 Camberwell Road, Camberwell,
Victoria 3124, Australia (a division of Pearson Australia Group Pty. Ltd.)
Penguin Books India Pvt. Ltd., 11 Community Centre, Panchsheel Park,
New Delhi – 110 017, India
Penguin Group (NZ), 67 Apollo Drive, Rosedale, Auckland 0632, New Zealand
(a division of Pearson New Zealand Ltd.)
Penguin Books (South Africa) (Pty.) Ltd., 24 Sturdee Avenue, Rosebank,
Johannesburg 2196, South Africa

Penguin Books Ltd., Registered Offices: 80 Strand, London WC2R 0RL, England

First published by Hudson Street Press, a member of Penguin Group (USA) Inc.

First Printing, November 2011
10   9   8   7   6   5   4   3   2   1

 REGISTERED TRADEMARK—MARCA REGISTRADA
HUDSON
STREET
PRESS

LIBRARY OF CONGRESS CATALOGING-IN-PUBLICATION DATA

Pillemer, Karl A.
   30 lessons for living : tried and true advice from the wisest Americans / Karl Pillemer.
      p. cm.
   Includes bibliographical references.
   ISBN 978-1-59463-084-2 (hbk. : alk. paper) 1. Older people—United States—Attitudes.
2. Old age. 3. Aging. 4. Happiness. 5. Conduct of life. I. Title. II. Title: Thirty lessons for
living.
   HQ1064.U5P55 2011
   305.260973—dc23   2011017113

Printed in the United States of America
Set in Adobe Garamond Pro
Designed by Catherine Leonardo

To Clare, Hannah, and Sarah, for teaching me
my most important lessons for living

CONTENTS

ACKNOWLEDGMENTS

THIS PROJECT TOOK PLACE over five years and involved collecting information from more than a thousand older Americans. Over that period of time, I received invaluable help, support, and encouragement from a large number of individuals and organizations. It is a pleasure to acknowledge them here.

I am most indebted to those I call in this book the "experts" on living, the people who donated their time and their thoughts freely and openly. There is no way to repay them for providing the raw material on which this book is based; I can only hope that I have conveyed their lessons for living as they would have wanted it done.

I am very grateful to the individuals who assisted in collecting the data. The Cornell University Survey Research Institute—led by Yasamin Miller, director, and Darren Hearn, manager—was a joy to work with. Special thanks are due to interviewers Vanessa Mc-Caffery, Chris Dietrich, Chelsea Fenush, and Curtis Miller, who cheerfully unlearned the rules of standardized survey research to have deep and intimate conversations with the interviewees, laughing and sometimes crying with them. Linda Finlay also conducted a number of in-depth interviews and contributed important insights throughout the project. Leslie Schultz carried out many complex management tasks, keeping the interviews and data files organized and easy to use.

I am indebted to past and present members of my research team who assisted in identifying interviewees, transcribing interviews, providing ideas, coding, and related tasks: Dr. Myra Sabir, Helene Rosenblatt, Emily Parise, Mimi Baveye, Dr. Rhoda Meador, Esther Greenhouse, and Noreen Rizvi, as well as the Cornell undergraduates who conducted pilot interviews for the study.

I would like to thank the many individuals and organizations who sought out and nominated elders for interviews. Dr. Kevin O'Neil and Sara Terry of Brookdale Senior Living produced, from their communities across the country, an extraordinary set of interviewees for the project. Dr. Mark Lachs and Dr. Cary Reid of the Division of Geriatrics and Gerontology at the Weill Cornell Medical College introduced me to interesting New Yorkers, as did Mary Ballin of the Irving Sherwood Wright Center on Aging. I am also grateful to the following individuals at the New York City senior centers that assisted with the project: Josie Piper, Central Harlem Senior Citizens Coalition; Chan Jamoona and Vidya Jamoona, United Hindu Cultural Council Senior Center; Julia Schwartz-Leeper, Riverdale Senior Services; Nancy Miller, Visions/Services for the Blind and Visually Impaired; and Bill Dionne, the Carter Burden Center for the Aging. They taught me an important lesson about aging: support your local senior center!

Other individuals provided excellent suggestions for interviewees. My undergraduate mentor, gerontologist Ruth Harriet Jacobs, offered not only advice on the book but a number of excellent interviewees. Rosalie Muschal-Reinhardt and Elly Katz pointed me toward interviewees involved in "Sage-ing" activities. David Pomeranz from the Hebrew Home for the Aged at Riverdale introduced me to a number of residents there. Staff from the Office for the Aging in a number of New York counties and the Cornell Cooperative Extension system helped in the search for the wisest elders.

Several individuals provided invaluable help by reviewing all or part of the manuscript. Peter Wolk and Risa Breckman far exceeded the duties of friendship by providing invaluable feedback at critical stages. Sheri Hall offered many insightful comments throughout the writing process.

I am immensely grateful to my agent, Janis Donnaud, who several years ago listened to a semicoherent phone call about my idea and told me that, yes, she did think there might be a book in there somewhere. Without her assistance, *30 Lessons for Living* would never have seen the light of day. I would also like to acknowledge my editor at Hudson Street Press, Caroline Sutton, whose insightful comments made the book much better.

Finally, writing this book proved to be a family affair to a greater extent than I had anticipated, from reading the manuscript to offering opinions on production details. My wife, Clare McMillan, lent both her extraordinary editorial skills and her unflagging support to the project. My daughters, Hannah Pillemer and Sarah Pillemer, and son-in-law, Michael Civille, read drafts and provided me with young people's perspectives on the lessons. I am also blessed with an extended family that includes people with many areas of expertise relevant to the book, including two physicians, a research dietician, a family therapist, and a developmental psychologist. For lengthy discussions as well as willingness to listen to my angst when needed, I am grateful to David Pillemer, Stephen Pillemer, Eric Pillemer, Jane Pillemer, Helen Rasmussen, and Julianna Pillemer.

A NOTE ON NAMES

ALL NAMES USED IN this book are pseudonyms and any resemblance to those of actual persons, living or dead, is entirely coincidental. Most names were created using a random name generator (yes, there is such a thing). In fact, one way to be absolutely certain that you are *not* in this book is to find your name mentioned in it.

30 LESSONS FOR LIVING

—— ❖ ❖ ❖ ——

CHAPTER 1

Who Are the Wisest Americans and What Can They Tell Us?

FINDING THE RIGHT MATE and staying happily married for your whole life. Raising children who turn out well and enjoy your company. Discovering work you love. Growing older gracefully and without anxiety. Avoiding major regrets. Reaching the end of life with a sense of completion and fulfillment. This may sound like a wonderful prescription for a life well lived. But where can we find the guidance we need to accomplish these goals in our lives?

If you picked up this book because the title caught your eye, you've probably asked yourself that question. And my goal in writing it has been to provide you with concrete, practical advice about how to make the most of your life in precisely those ways. But first I need to let you know who these "wisest Americans" are and what kind of a guide this is. As you will see, it's different from any kind of advice book you've read before. That's because it taps a unique source that has been around for millennia but is almost forgotten in contemporary society.

Americans seek advice with an appetite that seems to be insatiable. We watch televised "experts" in the hope of finding solutions to interpersonal problems, financial woes, and sexual dysfunction. We read advice columns and go to seminars. We consult self-improvement websites. And we buy books. There are more than thirty thousand self-help titles in print in the United States today, and it's estimated that Americans will spend close to one billion dollars buying them this year.

Let me make a confession: I am something of an advice junkie myself. I am the kind of person who goes directly to the self-help aisle in the megabookstore. For almost every topic I am interested in, you will find a relevant advice volume in my bookcase. My family has learned to ignore my reading aloud from the daily paper the latest tips on getting organized, reducing stress, investing for retirement, or whatever the problem of the day happens to be. I know I'm not alone in these activities—it seems like almost everyone is looking for answers to life's complex questions.

And yet as I observed all this searching, I felt something was missing. What credentials do the supposed gurus to the good life have? What entitles them to special authority when it comes to solving life's problems? And why, if we have so many professional advice givers, are so many people still so unhappy? The overflowing feast of advice seems to have left a lot of people pushing back from the table hungry.

Philosophers, psychologists, and spiritual leaders point toward the underlying discontent many Americans feel about the ways their lives are turning out. We live in the midst of plenty but always seem to want more. We feel that we do not have enough time, and yet we waste the precious time we have on video games, text messaging, reading about the lives of talentless celebrities, or earning more money to buy things we don't need. We always seem to be worrying—about our health, our children, our marriages, our jobs.

Where, I began to wonder, can we find advice that is based in lived reality, has stood the test of time, and offers a chance of genuinely helping us make the most of our lives? Six years ago, when I turned fifty, I realized that I deeply and urgently wanted an answer to that question. Turning fifty brings you into a new and interesting phase of life (at least it did for me). You still have one foot firmly placed in marriage, work, child rearing, and planning ambitiously for the future. But you also have a whiff of things to come. Your children are nearing adulthood and leaving home. You might have lost one or both parents. Your perfect health may be a bit less perfect.

But most important, you begin having a longer lifetime to look back on. And you find yourself *knowing* things. You see a twenty-three-year-old in the throes of romantic indecision, and you hear yourself saying: "I've been through that. Believe me, you'll feel better." You see two younger colleagues in a knock-down, drag-out battle over something trivial, and you say to a coworker your age: "Can you believe how worked up those guys are getting? What's the point?" For some experiences, the highs of success and the lows of failure aren't as high or low. There's a nascent sense of the long view, of individual events finding their place in a larger context. And maybe you start to feel a greater acceptance of others, a desire to slow down a bit, and an awareness of small pleasures in the present moment.

An idea began to percolate in my mind: maybe there is something about getting older that teaches you how to live better. A question dawned on me that gave birth to this project: Could we look at the oldest Americans as *experts on how to live our lives?* And could we tap that wisdom to help us make the most of our lifetimes?

I'm a bit embarrassed to say that this insight came as a surprise to me, because I have spent my career as a gerontologist: someone who studies people in life's "third age"—typically thought of as the period after age sixty-five. Over the past thirty years, I have conducted dozens of studies and published scientific articles on topics like the stress of taking care of parents with Alzheimer's disease, ways of helping elders deal with chronic pain and disability, and how to improve care in nursing homes. In my studies I have used rigorous methods, scientifically selected samples, and proven measures to try to understand the aging process. But I felt I was missing something nevertheless. Despite decades studying the problems of older people, I had a nagging suspicion that there was more they could tell me about how to live the good life.

Then one particular event pushed me firmly in a new direction and launched an effort that would occupy (some would say obsess) me for five years. It was a turning point, the importance of which I didn't realize immediately but which eventually led to *30 Lessons for Living.*

My work often takes me into nursing homes. I don't know how much time you have spent in nursing homes, but you can take my word for it that they aren't the happiest places on the planet. Although most provide good care, they have an institutional feel that depresses the spirits as you pass through the front door. Both the residents and the staff know that entering the home is a one-way street; for almost everyone, the only exit is the end of life. Nursing homes look after the sickest and most vulnerable people in our society, many of whom have lost their loved ones, their ability to care for themselves, and sometimes even their memories and sense of self.

On this particular day, a nurse I was chatting with said, "Do you have a minute? I'd like you to meet June Driscoll. I hear you like to meet interesting older people"—which I do—"and I've got one for you."

The room was typically institutional, with two beds. June, sitting in an armchair next to the window, turned at the nurse's greeting. I could see that June was thin, her face framed by a halo of cottony white hair. Her skin had the waxy translucency one sometimes sees in the very old. I knew from the nurse that June was a "total care" resident, requiring assistance with every activity of daily living, including the most personal. "Her vision is going," the nurse told me, "so stand close so she can see you." After nearly ninety years, June's body was in the final process of failing her.

The nurse's greeting was conventional: "How are you doing today?" But the answer had a dramatic effect on me. "Just fine!" June replied in a surprisingly strong voice. "Fine day so far! I've had my bath, lunch was good, and I'm getting ready to watch my program." Without a pause, she went on to ask the nurse about her toddler at home who had been ill for the past few days. Reassured that he was fine, June turned her attention to me. I don't know how else to put it: she seemed to be having a very good time.

I was intensely curious about where a cheerful attitude like hers came from, near the end of life and despite a host of physical problems. Maybe it was something special in the moment, but before I had time to think I found myself actually asking her that question. And June didn't seem surprised at all. She nodded in a friendly way and told me: "Well, it's like this. I was raised in what you could call a shack, with a dirt floor and no indoor bathroom. I had six kids, and my husband was partially disabled and in and out of work. I worked hard every day of my life until I was bone tired. I've been through the Depression, when we barely had enough to eat. Now here I am, in a place where I have a roof over my head, three square meals a day, and very nice people who take care of me. There's a lot to do here. I wake up and the sun is shining in the window. I'm alive, after all. I can hear. I can still see okay."

June sat forward a little. "Young man," she said—and I am not ashamed to admit that it was gratifying to be called "young man" at my age—"you will learn, I hope, that happiness is what you make it, where you are. Why in the world would I be unhappy? People here complain all the time, but not me. It's my responsibility to be as happy as I can, right here, today."

She repeated the last sentence, as if to make sure I understood the urgency of the insight: "It's my responsibility to be as happy as I can be, right here, today." Then, politely, she let me know that her show, a current events program, was coming on the television: "I like to keep up with things!" I thanked her for her time and took my leave.

I didn't go back to that nursing home, and I imagine that June Driscoll lived no more than a few months. But I found myself thinking, "What's *that* all about?" How can it be that someone at the end of life and beset with a host of physical problems would have such a positive and optimistic outlook?

And so I went on a quest for wisdom. I didn't search in the usual way, by traveling the world, finding a therapist, or taking up an esoteric religious practice. To find practical guidance for living, my answer was to search for *the life wisdom of older people*. And I was not disappointed.

I came to believe that the knowledge of America's elders can serve as an extraordinary guide to finding fulfillment when life gets difficult. Older people bring firsthand experience to the table. They have lived life and learned from it. Suddenly the answer seemed obvious: why not interview a large number of elders so others can take advantage of "the wisdom of crowds"? We know that large groups of people often prove smarter than a few elite pundits and are better at solving problems and making good decisions.

When you put together lots of older people who have lived rich and fulfilling lives and who are willing to share their life lessons with others, you have a unique source of guidance—one that can help Americans of all ages. Their wisdom makes them the true experts on living well, even when times get tough. Readers will find in this volume both practical solutions and assurance that it is indeed possible to overcome life's major challenges and to discover joy in the face of adversity.

Older Americans: The Experts on Living

We are on the verge of losing an irreplaceable natural resource. The inexorable process of human aging is depriving us of one of the most extraordinary groups of human beings that has ever lived: America's older generation. The last veteran of World War I has died; those of World War II are now in their eighties. The youngest children of the Great Depression have reached their late seventies. When this generation has passed, where will we go to recover the lessons they learned about life and the wisdom they can offer us about surviving and thriving in a difficult world? Each older person, as the interviews in this book demonstrate, is a storehouse of experience and guidance for how to live well. But as each of these lives winks out, the light it can shed is lost. Behind this book is a sense of urgency. It is predicated on a need to distill, preserve, and share what America's elders have to teach us about leading a happy, fulfilling life—before they are gone.

As the title of this book indicates, I believe our elders are the wisest Americans. Therefore throughout this book I use a special term for the people I talked with: "the experts." Why do I call them the experts on how to make the most of your life? I'll give you some good reasons.

Older people have one unique source of knowledge that the rest of us do not: *they have lived their lives.* They have been where younger people haven't. It's true that they may not be the quickest to program a DVD player, may prefer to face a bank teller in person than to use an ATM, and probably aren't up on the latest reality TV show. But they have the enormous advantage of life experience. Indeed people who have lived most of a long life are in an ideal position to assess accurately what "works" and what doesn't. It is precisely such expertise that I tapped for this book. A younger person simply can't know life as deeply and intimately as an older person does.

Another reason to listen to the experts' advice about living is that they are extraordinary people. America's elders have lived through experiences many of us today can barely imagine. Their limits have been tested by illness, failure, oppression, loss, and danger. It is precisely these situations that lead to transcendental wisdom. And America's elders have it to a greater degree than the rest of us because, on average, they have been pushed to the limit more than we have. They have survived these experiences, absorbed them, and gained invaluable insights from them.

Older people (and especially those in their seventies and beyond) have lived in a very different way from Americans today. They risked their lives in World War II, coming home with a widened view of the world but also deep scars. Some survived the Holocaust and others cheated death daily, fighting in the Resistance. Most grew up in times of sore deprivation—this has shaped their attitudes toward wealth and material goods. Their childhoods were sometimes beset with grim difficulties, and many of them experienced the horrors of war and poverty firsthand. But they also remember a time when the air and water were cleaner, when people didn't lock their houses, and when neighbors could be called on for help. They bring to contemporary problems and choices perspectives from a different time. This unique point of view can be enormously valuable as a lens through which to view our own lives.

Finally, there's one more reason why throughout this book I call America's elders "the experts" and why I refer to them as "the wisest Americans" in its title. Their unique perspective provides a much-needed antidote to conventional wisdom about the "good life" in contemporary American society. Conventional wisdom is what everybody knows—what the members of a society learn while they are growing up. Conventional wisdom is convenient because it provides guidance about how to live, offering up images of the good life and reinforcing the values of the culture. Ultimately, conventional wisdom becomes the basis for our identity and sense of self-esteem.

The experts' advice often upends contemporary conventional wisdom and points to an alternative. This alternative wisdom defies simple categorization: sometimes their insights are what we think of as liberal (the elders endorse religious tolerance, for example, and they reject materialistic worldviews) and sometimes conservative (such as proposing that marriage should be seen as a lifelong commitment). At times their viewpoint seems radically different from that of the young—this is true of their attitude toward time and how to spend it. But it is in this challenge to the conventional worldview of younger people that the true value of their wisdom lies. It can lead us to examine contemporary social conventions and make more conscious decisions about our own scripts for happiness.

This book is predicated on one idea: that the accumulated wisdom of America's elders—the experts—can serve as an excellent guide to life for people of all ages. The experts possess deep knowledge of just about every problem a human being can experience. You be the judge and see what the advice of over one thousand of the wisest Americans can tell you. As much as possible, I have let the experts speak for themselves, allowing you to hear the lessons they offer through direct quotes. I think you will find that the road map for life they provide will help you to take a new look at your own situation and to chose new ways of living that will make you happier.

Harvesting the Life Lessons of the Experts

Without boring you with technical detail, I'd like to tell you how the information in this book was collected. (A detailed appendix appears at the end of this book, for those of you who are interested.) My approach to gathering the information was to use methods that allowed people to speak their minds, telling their stories in rich detail (what social scientists refer to as "qualitative" research). I began by publicizing the project and inviting older people to send me their answers to the questions "What are the most important lessons you have learned over the course of your life?" and "If you were offering a younger person advice about how to live, what would you tell him or her?" To my surprise and delight, hundreds of letters came in from across the country, and many more people entered responses on a website created for the project.

Next I conducted a national survey of over three hundred people age sixty-five and over. This was a scientifically conducted survey in which respondents were selected at random and called on the telephone by trained interviewers. The survey began by asking them, in general, "What lessons have you learned in your life?" It then followed up by asking what respondents felt they had learned in specific domains, such as work and career, marriage, raising children, health, and religion and spirituality. They were also asked whether there were any problems or difficulties in their lives that had taught them valuable lessons, what core values and principles they lived by, and what advice they had about how to age successfully.

Finally, to get the most complete picture possible, detailed, in-depth interviews were conducted with approximately three hundred people from around the country and from many walks of life. I asked a range of individuals and organizations to suggest people over the age of sixty-five who they considered to be particularly wise. The nominated elders were encouraged to describe their views in great detail and to provide the life histories that formed the background to the lessons they'd learned. In all, well over one thousand older Americans answered the question, "What are the most important lessons you have learned over the course of your life?" You hold in your hands what they had to say.

What You Will Find Here

In collecting the data and writing this book, my primary goal was that the reader should find the information *useful*. The point was not to tell the life stories of older people—other books do that. I spent months reviewing, sorting, and categorizing the thousands of specific pieces of advice the experts offered on almost every imaginable challenge life can offer. I then distilled their perspectives on these issues, summing up what over a thousand people who had lived most of their lives saw as the advice they wished to offer to younger generations. As I combed through hundreds of pages of responses, the advice the experts offered fell naturally into six major themes. Within each of these themes, I have distilled five key lessons. That's what you will find in the following chapters: thirty lessons for living that you can begin using right away.

I start with what the experts advise us about getting and staying married, based on their total of about thirty thousand years of married life (many have been married for thirty, forty, fifty, or more years). We move then to their advice on finding a career you love and keeping it fulfilling; they've done everything from manual labor to writing poetry to occupying the CEO's office suite. Next we look at their lessons about child rearing, drawn from their collective experience raising around three thousand kids. I devote a chapter to an area in which no one would doubt their expertise: how to grow old fearlessly and well. Then the experts tackle a question that can save us all much inner turmoil: how to avoid having serious regrets throughout your life. The last five lessons take on the big picture: what do the experts know about how to make the most of life, remaining happy and fulfilled despite inevitable loss and illness?

So what do you have before you? Think of the thirty lessons for living as a road map. What, after all, is a road map built upon besides the combined experience of countless people who have traveled the terrain before? As you will see in this book, there are things about life—secrets, if you will—that are probably impossible for younger people to know firsthand. We need to consult those who have already traveled the roads, byways, dead ends, and unexpected detours to understand which directions our lives should take. You will not be reading the words of celebrities, popular pundits, TV preachers, twentysomething "lifestyle" critics, or paid motivational speakers. You will instead be reading the voice of experience from the oldest and wisest Americans—the experts. I think it may change your life. It did mine.

CHAPTER 2

❖ ❖ ❖

Great Together
Lessons for a Happy Marriage

Ruth Helm, 84

WHEN I WAS SIXTEEN, I met Joe—the love of my life.
My family had to leave Germany when I was a child in the
1930s, because of Hitler and the Nazis. So we came to New
York City. Well, my sister Ellen met her boyfriend, Tom, at
a club there. It was the type of café you had in Europe. And
we used to go there, the young women, and talk, play a
little cards with the boys, that kind of thing.

So one day my sister says to me, "Tomorrow, come

with us to the soccer game, Tom's going to play soccer." And that's where I met Joe for the first time, and we became good friends.

We were just friends when he went into the army in World War II. When Joe came back he got in touch with me and we saw each other. I was twenty. He always gave parties, he had a lot of friends, and everybody liked him. He invited me to his parties, and I'd bring my friends. He'd bring the boys. I'd bring the girls. And he was very nice.

One day he said, "You want to come dancing with me tonight?" "Oh no," I said, "with me you've got to make a date a week in advance." First of all, that was the style then. But besides that, you know why I didn't want to go with him? I liked him so much as a friend, I was afraid if I went on a date with him and he kissed me and I didn't like it, we wouldn't be able to be friends anymore. I didn't want to lose him as a friend.

So then he organized a New Year's party, and my friend Sarah and I went together. You know what he did? At midnight he managed to be right next to me. At midnight everybody kisses, you know. So it was twelve o'clock and he grabbed me and he kissed me. That night when I went home with Sarah I said, "I'm going to marry Joe!" That kiss! And he'd been wanting to do that for years.

Then we started dating and we never dated anybody else. It was just the two of us and in the end we got married. And we were married fifty-two years. He died—it's going to be ten years soon. Yes, he was the love of my life. He was my true love. Not that we didn't have fights, but we loved each other like crazy in every way—physically, mentally. We were great together.

*   *   *

MARRIAGE IN CONTEMPORARY SOCIETY presents a paradox. On the one hand, many believe that the institution of marriage is under severe, perhaps terminal, threat. Over the past half century, rates of marriage have fallen, people are waiting longer to get married, and divorce rates have increased, leading to the oft-cited statistic that around half of all U.S. marriages will end in divorce. For much of Western history, the family—consisting of husband, wife, and children—was a bulwark of society: the social institution that structured the private lives of most people. In contrast, nowadays four in ten children are born to unmarried mothers, and the majority of people live together before getting married, raising the question, Is that piece of paper really necessary?

There's a flip side to these sobering statistics, however. In popular culture marriage has certainly never gone out of style. And there's perhaps no more evocative summation of the reasons why than that of Ellie Banks in the 1950s film classic *Father of the Bride*: "Oh, Stanley. I don't know how to explain. A wedding. A church wedding. Well it's, it's what every girl dreams of. A bridal dress, the orange blossoms, the music. It's something lovely to remember all the rest of her life." Surveys in fact show that marriage is still the ideal for most people in American society. Among high school seniors, fewer than 10 percent say they do not expect to marry. Ultimately, 90 percent of Americans will wind up tying the knot.

Thus it appears that, despite current challenges, marriage is here to stay as an American institution and ideal. And this isn't a bad thing—in fact there is general consensus among family scholars that marriage is good for us. The noted family historian Stephanie Coontz sums up the research concisely: "Today married people in Western Europe and North America are generally happier, healthier, and better protected against economic setbacks and psychological depression than people in any other living arrangement." Married people enjoy higher incomes and greater emotional support. Perhaps the most compelling sign that there is something to marriage is the proportion of divorced people who remarry (around 75 percent, and most of those within four years after the divorce)—a phenomenon that has sardonically been labeled "the triumph of hope over experience."

So here we have the paradox. Most people want to get married and there is considerable evidence that marriage has a wide range of benefits. But too often the joy that accompanies the wedding celebration turns sour, and nearly half of the couples who stand at the altar in hopeful excitement find themselves starting over after the trauma of divorce. Scholars are not sure about what makes one marriage last until "death do us part" while another ends up on the rocks. There are a number of theories, but clear research-based advice is lacking. Indeed the divorce rate itself shows how little good guidance there is.

In this chapter we'll look at what the wisest Americans advise us about finding a life partner and staying married (remember that many of them have been married for decades). When we contrast the marital experience of the experts with that of younger people, we see that the process of entering into marriage was the same for them as for younger generations—except where it was different. The uncertainty and anxiety (Will I ever find my true love?) were the same as they are today, as is the exhilaration of the first meeting, the early flirtation, and the excitement of the daily discovery of new facets to the beloved person. However, their experience stands in sharp contrast to modern courtship with its Internet dating, singles bars, starter marriages, and "hookups."

I've distilled the experts' advice into five lessons for marriage.

Throughout these lessons, I often refer to "marriage" and "finding a marriage partner." That wording reflects their advice, because few of the elders were in long-term unmarried partnerships. I recognize, however, that there are approximately five million cohabiting couples in the United States. For some individuals the decision to live together represents a pivotal commitment in their lives, sometimes akin to marriage. Further, many states deny same-sex couples the right to legal marriage. So depending on your situation, you can take the recommendations for "marriage" as advice for "entering a committed relationship"; the lessons apply in both cases.

The First Lesson:
Marry Someone a Lot like You

I asked hundreds of older Americans what is most important for a long and happy marriage, and their advice was just about unanimous: opposites may attract, but they may not be the best for lasting marriages. You will recall my warning that some of the experts' lessons are controversial and won't sit well with everyone. But it's important to convey to you exactly what they told me—especially when nearly everyone endorsed the same principle. Based on their long experiences both in and out of love relationships, their first lesson is this: *you are much more likely to have a satisfying marriage for a lifetime when you and your mate are fundamentally similar.*

Most important, the experts believe that marriage is vastly more difficult with someone whose orientation and approach to life is different from yours. There are many ways partners can be similar, but the experts focus on one dimension in particular: *similarity in core values.*

Now, I have talked to many people entering into relationships over the years, and I have heard all kinds of reasons for falling in love. For people in their twenties, reasons include things like the love interest having a lively sense of humor, making good money, and of course being nice looking. Searching my memory, I failed to come up with a single example of someone saying, "Oh, I'm seeing the most wonderful person. The best thing is that we share the same core values!" The experts' advice, however, is that values are precisely what we should look for if we want a long, happy marriage. Here's where the view from old age is uniquely powerful. Instead of standing at the beginning of the winding trail, barely able to see around the first bend, the experts know the entire terrain; what makes the long journey easy and what makes it difficult or impossible. That's where shared values come in.

Take Emma Sylvester, who at eighty-seven has been married for fifty-eight years. As she puts it with a smile, "It's quite an achievement."

I DIDN'T KNOW IT when I got married, but in retrospect I know it's important to have the same basic values. In other words, if you're a free spender, marry somebody who understands that. If you're frugal, you need to marry somebody who understands that, because money is one of the stumbling blocks in marriages. And fortunately we have the same values on most things.

Because of this, we really don't argue. And we really don't agonize over things. We come to our decisions just by realizing that we usually have the same goals. We both believed in education. We wanted to be moral according to society's standards, to raise our children to be good citizens, and to be responsible in terms of finances.

The key phrases here are "we really don't argue" and "we really don't agonize over things." Arguments emerge over apparently trivial issues, the experts tell us, because they really reflect underlying values. Whether the wife purchases an expensive golf club or the husband a new electronic toy is not the core issue in what can become a monumental fight. It is, rather, the deeper attitude toward what money means, how it should be spent, and whether the financial interests of the couple are more important than indulging an individual whim. Similarity in core values serves as a form of inoculation against fighting and arguing.

Keith Koon, seventy-four, is a very reflective person who has thought extensively about values. "In my teens, I connected very closely with Zen, and I believe in connecting heart and mind and being authentic. And as you live life, that connection just gets deeper and deeper."

In his first marriage, he told me: "We found out that we were just not for each other. We had whole different backgrounds, different perspectives. We came to the point where we asked, 'What's the point of this?' I understood this in my second marriage, and it's been wonderful for twenty-four years. It's based this time on compatibility and understanding one another's values." Echoing other value similar couples, Keith told me, "We've never had a fight. In other words, there's no meanness, there are no power struggles, no 'my way is the right way,' or those kinds of things."

Ben Santorelli is seventy-five years old. Born and bred in the Bronx, his family took years to recover from the Depression. They lived in rooms behind his father's store. "My brother and I slept on the sofa bed in the living room. I never thought I was deprived. It was a very happy family. We had a big extended family, lots of relatives living around." He loves retirement, filling it with a wide range of interests and activities. The greatest joy of his life, however, is his marriage, and it is based on similarity.

MY WIFE AND I have always considered ourselves extremely lucky in what has happened in our life, almost as if

we had a guardian angel. We met through work. I had
started in September, and after the first couple of days I was
there I noticed the secretary working there, and I thought
she was very nice looking. And, as I say, my guardian angel
was there. I started taking her to a class we were both taking
at the same time. Then we started eating out together, and
one thing led to another. We started dating, and eventually
I proposed to her. So that was it, and she accepted.

It felt like it was meant to be. We were very similar in
many respects. I really enjoyed many cultural things. I used
to go to Shakespeare in the Park. I used to go to the ballet
and the theater. So I wanted someone who could enjoy
those things with me. I was very interested in classical music, and I was delighted that she loved it too. Well, we just
loved each other. We're like two peas in a pod. We just
agreed on so many things. We also share values about poli-
tics, everything.

You may be wondering whether the emphasis on similarity in
marriage is a conservative, stick-to-your-own-kind mentality. However, this viewpoint cut across all groups: economic, political, geo-
graphical, and racial. For example, April Stern, seventy-one, is far
to the left among the experts, raised in a socialist household in the
1940s and heavily influenced by feminism and the 1960s counter-
culture movement. Nevertheless, when asked about the secret of a
happy marriage she eloquently articulated the importance of similarity.

April and her husband, Steve, were married for forty-seven
years until Steve's death a year before the interview. April is a highly
respected community leader who directed several local organizations and Steve was a well-known local psychotherapist. They were
deeply in love throughout their relationship, and April is still ad-

justing to widowhood: "When I was twenty I was already very much in love with Steve. I know now that I can keep going, since his death, but I get a little weepy, still, talking about him." And life with Steve was very good. "I think we modeled a good marriage, our children even talked about that as being important to them," says April.

IT SOUNDS SIMPLE, BUT you have to like each other. Be friends, try to get past the initial heaving and panting and make sure there's a real friendship underneath that. I don't think you have to have identical interests, but you've got to have shared values. That is quite important. That was critical. Yeah, I think values are probably the most important thing.

And we both loved certain kinds of things. We both loved movies, good movies, and part of our courtship involved staying up all night and figuring out what an Ingmar Bergman film really meant. We both loved to read, and we loved to talk about what we'd read.

In spite of having met in the sixties, we happened to have a very strong commitment to monogamy and to trust, and that was very important to us. I think in part, Steve, as a clinician, had all these people trucking into his office who had tried other ways of walking in the world that hadn't worked and there were just disastrous situations. And I know that for some people that wasn't true. But I think it left us with a real commitment to being honest and true to each other.

When asked what kinds of values they shared, April replied:

POLITICAL VALUES, FEELINGS ABOUT not living in an ostentatious way, about commitment to other people, and our own commitments. We both had different specific commitments, but strong commitments in feeling that we owed something back, that our lives were going pretty well and we owed something back, not only of resources, but of time. We both loved to travel, and we had a sense of adventure. We liked the same people, and I think that's important. Very seldom did we disagree about friends. And parenting, of course. We had very similar values in terms of our kids and what we wanted for them.

She paused for a moment to consider, and then added with a wistful smile:

AND YOU HAVE TO have, I think, a similar sense of humor. That was a very important part of our life together. In fact, just two weeks before he died, we were talking one night, and he said something and I just dissolved in laughter, and he looked at me so self-satisfied and said, "I can still make you laugh after all these years!" And he could.

Of course, there is a catch: to ensure shared values one must know what one's own values are. John Fordham, eighty-three, has been married to his wife, Elaine, for thirty-three years. When asked what the secret to a long, happy marriage was, he responded: "Well, I think that one should know oneself. And then I suppose there's a semiconscious table of attitudes and values that one uses to find kindred spirits." He explained that you should begin by taking an inventory of what you value and what you believe in. Only then can you understand what would make another person compatible. "Because, by contrast, someone who doesn't seem to fit in with your own outlook—it becomes an issue. This is going to be the closest relationship you will have, except maybe parent-child.

You've got to make sure your values align, and to do that you need to understand what's important to you."

Gerald Hendrix, eighty-two, whom we will get to know better in the chapter on work, approached this subject in a concrete, methodical way (as he does in all domains of his life).

I THOUGHT THIS OUT carefully before I entered into marriage. I was married happily for forty-four years, and I lost my first wife to cancer. I remarried a wonderful woman, so I've had two very good, fulfilling marriages. And I did the same thing in both cases. I sat down with both of my girlfriends at the time, and I made a list of the seven or eight things that I valued and that I wanted to have from the relationship. Even in my first marriage I did this, which would have been sixty years ago. And I asked them both if that was agreeable. I said, if it isn't, I understand, and you can take a pass on me. But in both cases they said yes.

I asked for some examples of what was on the lists.

OKAY, ONE WAS "FAMILY oriented," because I value family very highly. I found out that I want someone who is "touchy"—I want someone who is not afraid to be touched and who's not afraid to touch. That's very important, and I'm not talking about sex. I'm talking about touching. Those were two of the things I asked right off the bat. A third was the value of independence. That's part of my freedom. Without that, I'm not me. These are lifestyle things. And it worked. At least it worked for me, with the two marriages. I've been supremely happy.

Do you need a list? Maybe not. But it clearly makes sense to explore one another's values while you are in the process of committing to a relationship. Ask the question, Do we believe the same things in life are important? The experts recommend that at some point, after things get serious, you discuss this issue to make sure your core values are as similar as possible. And if a problem develops in a relationship, they suggest that value differences are likely to be at the heart of it.

The wisdom of the experts is highly consistent with research findings over the past several decades. Social scientists who study marriage look for two things over the long term: marital stability (how long the marriage lasts) and marital quality (the sense of satisfaction and well-being partners experience). And these researchers, in time-honored social-scientific fashion, substitute for "similarity" a more specialized term: "homogamy." Homogamous marriages involve similar partners, whereas heterogamous marriages involve couples who differ in important characteristics. (Feel free to drop these terms at cocktail parties and amaze your friends.)

The research findings are quite clear: marriages that are homogamous in terms of economic background, religion, and closeness in age are the most stable and tend to be happier. Sharing core values has also been found to promote marital stability and happiness. So the experts are in the scientific mainstream when they urge you to seek a partner who is similar to you in important ways. But what should we do with this information?

In trying to act on this advice, we come up against a dilemma. On the one hand, the experts are as unanimous as we will ever see them on any issue. No matter their socioeconomic background, their religious heritage, their race or ethnicity, or their political leanings, they agree: finding someone who is similar in upbringing, general orientation, and values is the single most important component of a long and satisfying marriage. On the other hand, we live in a pluralistic society that increasingly values diversity, breaking down old barriers, and understanding and appreciation of differences. Is there a conflict here?

The message to take away from this lesson allows for both perspectives. The experts (like the social scientists) don't tell you unconditionally not to marry someone who is different from you but with whom you are deeply in love. They simply want everyone to recognize that if we marry people very dissimilar to ourselves, and in particular with divergent values, we are much more likely to face complex challenges in married life. According to the experts, in the face of objective differences (such as race or economic background), shared values and outlook on life will go a long way to promote both the quality and stability of a marriage.

One last piece of advice from the experts before we leave this lesson. We have seen that they believe a marriage is unlikely to last without similarity between the partners. But what about taking a leap of faith under the assumption that you can change your partner *after* you're married? This idea formed the basis of a hit Broadway musical, *I Love You, You're Perfect, Now Change*—the title says it all.

The experts are as clear about this scenario as can be: *forget about it!* According to them, entering into a marriage with the goal of changing one's partner is a fool's errand, one that will doom the marriage before it starts.

Allison Hanley, seventy-two, was married for thirteen years; the experience had such a profound effect on her that she never remarried. Her advice to younger people is as follows:

I WOULD SAY GET to know the person well and don't marry very young. I married too young, and in retrospect it would have been better for me and I would have been happier if I had been a little bit older and had a stronger sense of myself. I thought that I could make some changes in the person that I married, and unfortunately I wasn't able to do that. Once I was in the marriage I became pregnant almost immediately. I realized that it was going to be very difficult to extricate myself, for financial reasons as well as my own strong family values. That's something that I've learned along the way—that I can never change anyone. I can only change myself.

Tina Oliver, eighty-eight, has had a lot of experience with marriage. Not only was she happily married for forty-seven years, but she has observed her five children get and stay married. In addition she has spent her time volunteering with young people and has keenly observed their attempts at courtship and forming lasting relationships.

Tina spoke with one of our wonderful young interviewers. At one point Tina asked whether she had a boyfriend—she did—and whether they planned to get married (this kind of thing happened quite frequently with our outgoing interviewers). Our staffer said, "It could happen. Hard to say, the way things are going right now. I don't know for sure." Tina replied:

UNLESS YOU'RE SURE, DON'T! And you're not going to change him. If he's got his ways about him and if you don't like those ways, don't even think about it, because he's not going to change. It's at least twenty years that he's been in this rut, doing what he's doing, so he's not changing. It's very, very rare that a person changes much after marriage.

So before entering into marriage, you should examine what you expect to start changing about your mate once the honeymoon is over. Then ask yourself what it will mean if those things can't be changed. Because in the experts' view change is unlikely to happen. Indeed, you will have much greater success in changing your own feelings and behavior than in changing your partner's. Marriage is difficult enough, the experts tell us, so why make it even more difficult by choosing a partner who has attitudes or behaviors you can't tolerate? If you are entering into a permanent relationship based on the intention of change, you are on the wrong track.

The Second Lesson:
Friendship Is as Important as Romantic Love

In interviews with the experts, a very common response to the question "What's the secret to a long, happy marriage?" was essentially, "I married my best friend." Similarly, from those whose marriages did not succeed, I often heard, "Well, we were good at love, but we never learned how to be friends." In our culture, however, we are schooled to differentiate between friendship and romantic love. Take the iconic film *When Harry Met Sally*, which has become a symbol of the gap between the roles of friend and romantic partner. Indeed, television shows like *Will & Grace* and *Sex and the City* popularize the view that cross-sex friendship works best (or only) when one of the friends is gay. After marriage, a distinction develops between one's friends and one's spouse: two separate social categories that have different functions.

What are the special qualities of friendship? There's a lightness to it in contrast with marriage. We look forward to being with friends, we relish their company, we relax with them, we share common interests, and usually we talk. In contrast, we all encounter people who do not feel they can talk easily to their spouse (next time you are out for a fancy dinner observe the couples who manage only a few uncomfortable words over two hours). What the experts suggest is that you look for the qualities of a friend—the capacity to comfortably "hang out"—in the person you choose to marry. Or as one of the experts told me: "Think back to the playground when you were a kid. Your spouse should be that kid you wanted most to play with!"

The experts' point is this: when selecting a mate, don't let love blind you to the need for friendship. The truth is that somewhere along the line the heart-pounding, romantic thrill will become more muted (although we all hope it doesn't disappear). This is where the lens of experience becomes especially useful. The experts have seen in their own married lives a transition from the initial thrill of romantic attraction and—many were honest about it— overwhelming sexual desire to the stage when other things *must* become as or more significant. No matter how important the image of being swept off one's feet by true love, the experts caution you to ask, "What's next?" Will you wake up next to the same person for five or six decades and still find a person you like as well as love?

Nicole Ambriz, seventy, grew up in a household where her parents were definitively *not* friends. "As I grew up, I heard the conflicts. That was something that always stuck with me, and I just didn't want that conflict in my marriage or for my kids." She was therefore motivated to work hard in her married life when it was needed. "We realized after about twelve years that we were basically just existing. We got up, went to work, came home, cooked dinner—blah, blah, blah. The normal, everyday, run-of-the-mill thing."

Nicole and her husband sought out Marriage Encounter, a program that helps to revitalize long-term marriages. "I would say that is when we truly learned how to communicate and consider each other's feelings," says Nicole. "And we carried that on in our home and in our marriage." Her most important lesson from a half century of married life is this:

YOU HAVE TO BE friends first—that's what I didn't know—and you have to be willing to work on it. When we got married forty-nine years ago, it was the thing to do by the time you were twenty. Today that's not the case. And I have a lot of respect for young people who wait until they're twenty-five, thirty years old because the world is so different. We have spoken to young couples and we tell them, "You need to be good friends first and respect each other. Love comes and it grows if you are friends for one another."

Patty Banas, eighty, is one of the experts who made a go of a first marriage when young, divorced, and then "got it right" in her very happy second marriage. She too had one straightforward recommendation:

BE SURE THAT YOU'RE really good friends. That is the most important thing. All the romance and the bells and the whistles are all very nice, but it doesn't last. Be sure that you're very good friends.

In the experts' view, you should marry your friend and, if possible, your best friend. Quite literally, they suggest you consider what you would like in a lifelong friend and look for that in a potential spouse. As a relationship is moving into a serious phase, questions couples can and should discuss are: If we weren't in love, would be friends? And if we, as most couples do, downshift to something other than heart-thumping passion, what is there that will keep us together? (Hint: the answer should *not* be kids.) The answer is friendship, and if you don't have it, don't get married—it's that simple. As Marco Esteban, ninety, put it:

> ROMANCE AND LOVE ARE not the same, a lesson that experience teaches you. Romantic love, from what I've seen, is an insufficient condition for a successful marriage. What is thought to be love, at the outset of a marriage, is generally a mirage, for love develops slowly in marriage and continues to do so throughout its life. First there is intense physical attraction. Then there is joy of sharing similar activities and interests.

The Third Lesson: Don't Keep Score

In the interviews for this book, I sometimes needed to go on what I'd call a "drilling exploration" to understand the experts' lessons. Because sometimes the elders would sum up a complex area in a single phrase, and I had to drill down to find out the underlying significance. In a few cases—like the one I'm going to tell you about—so many people used the same expression that it seemed like a litany. Toward the end of the project, I could have almost lip-synched the responses to my question about what makes for a long and satisfying marriage: "Well, it's a lot of give and take." "Both partners have to be prepared to give and take." "You can't just give or just take, it has to be both."

This statement appeared self-evident to many of the experts, but it wasn't to me. When asked for an example or clarification, a frequent answer was, "Well, you know—give and take, right?" What was the basis for this insight, and why was it so important? I discovered the answer in a serendipitous way when Alvin Baker, an eighty-seven-year-old who had been married for sixty-three years, was asked, "So by that you mean that marriage has to be a fifty-fifty kind of thing, right? A fifty-fifty proposition?"

He nearly bellowed his disagreement—that was precisely *not* what he was saying. "Don't consider a marriage a fifty-fifty affair! Consider it 100 percent or even 110 percent—that's to allow for the lack of objectivity about our own 100 percent. It's got to be mutual."

Okay . . . Maybe I was slow on the uptake. It's definitely not fifty-fifty; it's more like 100 percent. But 100 percent of what? He went on: "The only way you can make a marriage work is to have both parties give 100 percent all the time." It began to make sense: you can't be calculating 50 percent in, 50 percent back. The attitude has to be one of giving freely. And if you start keeping score, you are already in trouble.

Sue Bennett, eighty-six, was married for sixty years. Her marriage had its ups and downs in the early years. She told me that she married too young and that she and her husband wanted very different things. As a result, the couple separated for several years but then reconciled and overcame their initial problems. She elaborated on the "more than fifty-fifty principle":

WELL, MARRIAGE IS NOT a fifty-fifty situation. It sometimes can be 90 percent to 10 percent. It depends on the situation. You have to keep giving a lot. You have to understand where the other person is coming from—put yourself in his or her shoes. And you have to have peace in the family. So you just decide, well, okay, this is it. You give in. And I've learned this through experience. There are times when you give and times when he gives—you can't sit around counting up who gets what.

For long-term success, couples have to orient themselves to giving *more* than they get. If both partners engage in the relationship with the goal of offering more to their partner than they receive, both benefit immensely. This is the advantage of true cooperation: both individuals are contributing to a *relationship*, the benefits of which transcend immediate interests on a given day. What couples must avoid—if they wish to remain together as long as the experts—is keeping score regarding who is getting more and who is getting less. This kind of economic attitude is one we would use, say, with a vending machine: if I put in my dollar, I will get a candy bar of equal value. According to the experts, this approach does not work in marriage.

Crystal Gullett's story is a good example. Crystal is young by expert standards, at just sixty-seven years old. Her varied experiences and her ability to reflect back on her life helped me to understand the issue of the "more than fifty-fifty marriage." Crystal, unfortunately, had no good model for a happy marriage; she describes her own family as "dysfunctional" to such an extent that she decided not to have children for fear of reproducing the unhappy dynamics. She also waited until she was thirty-five to get married, wanting to make sure she felt resolved about her traumatic early life and her ability to fully participate in a marriage.

When she wed her husband, Todd, Crystal entered into a family with five children, which was a difficult adjustment. "When rumor got around that I had married a man with five children, people were coming up to me going 'Oh my God!' and walking away. I was thinking: 'What's going on here? Why does everyone feel sorry for me all of a sudden?'" But Crystal did adjust, and she epitomizes the lesson that marriage is more than a calculated balance of give and take.

I CAN'T IMAGINE BEING married to anybody else. I'm married to a very special person and I feel very fortunate. Neither one of us is waking up in the morning and saying, "Am I getting what I need out of this?" Instead we're waking up saying, "What can I do for him?" or "What can I do for her?"

For example, my husband's gone through retirement and that was very difficult at first. He didn't know who he was. The phone wasn't ringing, so his sense of his own usefulness was very tenuous for a while. He found new things to do, but for a few years I think he was pretty depressed and floating around. I remember thinking, "Okay, now I need to wake up in the morning and think: he really needs something. He needs a little extra right now." And he's very much the same way for me.

When I had cancer, he was amazing, and I never felt frightened or abandoned. He can really be Mr. Super Caregiver. He was just like "I'm retired and this is going to be my full-time job." I was in the hospital twenty-five times or something during a year, and he drove up and drove back. I used to worry because you just disintegrate, but he was fine. He wasn't grossed out or anything. So this is how it goes. It goes up and down like this. Because there are times when one person is taking and needing, and then it's the other person.

I came to focus on the fifty-fifty fallacy because it resonated so strongly with the experts. A number of them used vivid imagery to illustrate this idea, which was sometimes otherwise difficult to express. An image that predominated was that of a team, used to portray the notion of a marriage in which both partners have the other's interests so much at heart that they "pull together" as one, lightening the load of life's difficulties because of their unified effort.

There are experts, and there are sages. Albert Folsom, eighty, is a true sage. I loved listening to him, basking in the presence of a truly wise person. Born in 1930 in the midst of the Great Depression, he grew up in a small hamlet in New York State. His father ran a general store, and Albert helped there as well as tending to the family's livestock. The lesson he took with him from childhood is the need for a family to work as a team.

When I asked Albert his marital status, he replied, "I'm married fifty-nine years to a very good wife. A good wife will make you, not break you. So I guess I was fortunate. Instead of worrying about who is winning and who is losing in a marriage, the key is working together, unconcerned about that kind of thing."

Albert then provided an image that reveals the core of expert wisdom about marriage.

WELL, THERE'S A LOCAL museum here in town. In it there's a life-sized statue of a team of work horses obviously pulling a large load, both of them laying heavily into the harness. And at our last anniversary the kids asked us, "How do you characterize or consider your marriage?" I said, "Go look at the sculpture, that team of horses. Both of them laying into the harness together." And written underneath it is, "As of One Mind." That sculpture characterizes, in my mind, our marriage. We came through some very hard times. There were times when we didn't know if we were going to make it. We've undergone fires and disasters and hailstorms and some very bad times. We not only survived them but we improved on the situations. But we did it together. If one person goes off and thinks he's going to do it by himself, it isn't going to work.

The last word on this topic goes to Antoinette Watkins, eighty-one, who in a piece of advice encapsulates the idea that marriage is not about keeping score.

I TALK WITH MY kids about marriage, and here is one little jewel that I pass along to them. When you wake up in the morning, think, "What can I do to make her day or his day just a little happier?" The idea being that you need to turn toward each other, and if you focus on the other person even just for five minutes when you first wake up, it's going to make a big difference in your relationship. You need to work out a way to support each other and work together as a team—then that's likely to really work for many years. So start each day thinking about what you can give that special person in your life.

I tried this one myself—and it works. Mornings in my house tend to be rushed, and with two busy people there's a temptation to look out for oneself, especially when stress gets the better of you. I'm often the culprit in putting my needs first: Can we leave when it fits my schedule? Can I stay late today while you go to the grocery store? As a result, an undercurrent of irritation builds up by the time you are out the door. I don't spend five minutes, like Antoinette suggests, but I do try to ask myself quickly, "What can I do to make her day a little happier?" If leaving fifteen minutes later or picking up the milk on the way home accomplishes that, why not do it? It definitely puts a different cast on the day.

The Fourth Lesson:
Talk to Each Other

In looking at your marriage, the experts suggest you ask one key question: Can you talk with your spouse? And can you talk with him or her about anything? Or are there hot spots that are off-limits for conversation as a couple? It may work out if one partner declares a minor topic off-limits (new phone apps, shoe sales, or any interactive video game, for example). But as a rule, the experts believe your partner simply must be someone you can talk to. Indeed the most frequent source of "buyer's remorse" in the experts' marriages was finding that a spouse just couldn't or wouldn't communicate.

Russell Lockwood is a delightfully opinionated eighty-five-year-old who has enjoyed a successful thirty-seven-year marriage. He works to keep the marriage lively—he still makes sure to play an April Fools' Day joke on his wife every year. (She tries as well, he says, "But she's not as good at it as I am.") He was raised in an era when husbands and wives didn't tend to communicate openly, and one of his most important life lessons is not to replicate such relationships.

WELL, I THINK A happy marriage is going to happen if you sit and talk about things. You can't let them boil up inside you, and then all of a sudden it blows up. So if something comes to mind and you feel like it's been bugging you, then you need to have it out, to talk about it. In other words, you've got to put the fire out when it first starts. It's something you should learn when you're dating. And it doesn't take too long to find out whether you can communicate with a person or not. If a marriage gets to the point where you can't discuss things, then you will have two unhappy people.

Where is communication most important? The experts agreed that one thing all couples need to do—if they want to remain married as long as the experts have—is learn to communicate about conflicts. More specifically, we all need to *learn how to fight*. Fights are inevitable; it's how we handle them that matters.

Dora Bernal is very funny. She was born and raised in the Bronx, and has the accent to prove it. When asked about marriage, she said, "In this old head, you know, there's too much there now to remember. We forget everything. Between my husband and me, we have one head. I'm eighty-six years old. My husband's an old man—he's eighty-seven." So you're not old yet, but he is? "That's right! And we're only married sixty-seven years!"

When asked about the advice she has for younger people about marriage, Dora talked about fighting:

WELL, THE ONLY THING I can really think of is this: just because you have a fight, it's not the end of things—you know what I'm saying? After all, there're two people living together, coming from different families, different upbringings. Even if the religion is the same, you're two different people. And if you fight, you have to recognize, "Oh well, so what? We had a fight." Ten minutes later you forget about it. As you get older, it becomes five minutes. Today people are, "Oh I had a fight," and they act like it was the end of the world. You just have to move on. There's at least two a week in this house! If you want to stay married, so you fight—big deal. How bad can it be?

So we have to get used to fights. Maybe that word is too strong for some couples, but even those who don't "fight" have disagreements. And it is in communication around disagreements, arguments, and differences of opinion that one secret to a long marriage lies. You've just heard someone in a great marriage that has lasted sixty-seven years (one of the longer ones among the experts) tell you cheerfully that she and her husband fight twice a week. It's not the fighting; it's how you deal with it.

It is therefore not surprising that the experts have worked out creative ways of talking through disagreements before they get to the knock-down, drag-out level. There wasn't any one method endorsed by all the elders. But they did have suggestions for how to communicate when things get tense, whether you call it a spat, a tiff, or a quarrel.

Tip 1: If you are having trouble discussing something, get out of the house.

Gary Surber, seventy-five, suggests that a change of scene can help you communicate about a disagreement.

AS PROBLEMS COME UP, as they do, of various types—many times it's finances—you can't give up on the relationship. Remember, this is the same person that you married, that you loved all your life. You should continue to try to work out the problems. But whatever it may be, I find that it's better to talk about problems that you can't seem to come to grips with when you're out of your own home. When you're in your own home, you're in the same atmosphere where the problems are going on. So you should go somewhere where you can talk—maybe it would be in the park, a restaurant, or somewhere else. We've done that when we needed to. I'm not sure why that works better, but it does.

Tip 2: Find a way to blow off steam, and then engage with your partner.

Antoinette Watkins found that writing helped defuse conflicts and increased her ability to discuss them.

> WHEN I BECAME TERRIBLY upset, I would sit down and write long letters to my husband, put them aside, read them the next day—and then throw them away. But it was a good idea to write it out. I think the big thing is to vent these things out of yourself, and you can do that in many ways. I found that writing helped.

Lydia McKeon, seventy-three, similarly advises couples to step back when they are angry, rather than engaging in the heat of the moment. Here's her creative solution:

> EVERY COUPLE NEEDS TO think of a way to let off steam by themselves, before they yell at one another. Now, we had some animals—horses and sheep and such like. What I would do was just leave and go out to the barn and pace around and talk to the animals, talk to the sheep. Of course they were always glad to see me, and they couldn't talk back. And then after a half hour or so, when I could just yell all I wanted to out there, I'd come back in. My husband had a big garden where he would go and do the same thing. You have to try to cool down. And while you're cooling down, you can yell as much as you want at animals, plants, or

whatever's out there, and they're not going to talk back to you. It worked for us.

So consider yelling at plants, farm animals, inanimate objects—rather than your spouse.

Tip 3: Watch out for teasing.

Ben Santorelli and his wife eliminated one way of relating that they found dangerous, a strategy that could be emulated by many couples:

> AFTER WE GOT MARRIED, we went through sort of a teasing phase, and it was getting out of hand. So we made a pact that we wouldn't tease the other person at all, and it really helped. It can degenerate into something nasty, teasing. So we just stopped it. I may have been the worst one, the bigger tease. I'm kind of a jokester, and maybe I thought it was funny. But it digs a little too deep. And then she would probably retaliate. It certainly changes the other person's attitude after they get teased. Looking back, that was an important moment, a turning point for us—to stop teasing. And it really cleared the air. It was wonderful.

Tip 4: Let your partner have his or her say.

The experts found making an effort to listen, and to clearly show your partner that you are listening, a major way to defuse conflict. I admit that this is one of my own flaws in marriage—shutting up long enough to hear my wife's perspective. So I tried the advice for listening, and found it truly helpful.

Here's eighty-two-year-old Natalie Buzzell's tip:

I LEARNED, WHEN YOU'RE communicating, to really listen to what the other person is saying. Before getting married, I had been single for quite a while—twenty-seven years. I was used to running my own life. I thought I knew all the answers. When my husband would talk, instead of listening to him I would be thinking what to say in reply, to contradict or to reinforce what I was trying to say. That is not the best thing when you communicate. You've really got to listen and let them have their say. When they're done, ask, "What would you want?" or "What do you think would be the right thing to do?" When I was in my twenties, I had all the answers. Now that I'm in my eighties, I'm not so sure my answers are always right.

Mark and Brenda Minton, both seventy-two, created a more formal way to make sure both parties get heard. I've tried this too, although the being quiet part is usually a struggle for me.

THERE'S ONE PARTICULAR TECHNIQUE that has worked for us, and we still practice it when the need arises. One person has the floor for five minutes, ten minutes, whatever you agree to. During that time, they offer what they are feeling. One party gets that for five minutes, and the other person listens and then repeats what was said until the first person agrees and says, "Yes, you got it right." Then you do it the other way. This slows down the exchange. It makes it much more likely that you really hear what the other person's hurts are and what their intentions are, because you have to be able to repeat it back. Then you get your turn to do the same. It opens things up more fully than standing around and wondering what's going on with the other person.

April Stern suggests "letting go." She offers a very useful tip for deciding who should let what go:

> IT'S IMPORTANT TO LET some things go, to figure out what matters and what really doesn't matter. There was one thing that we came to early on that really stayed with us—it was a very novel concept. If we were in some sort of struggle over something, we would stop and say, "Which one of us is this more important to?" And when we could figure that out, the other one found it so much easier to let go. But we needed to consciously stop and figure it out.

The Fifth Lesson:
Don't Just Commit to Your Partner—Commit to Marriage Itself

There's one big difference between couples my age and younger and those seventy and older: the seventy-plus group expected to marry for life, and the stigma of divorce kept people together during rough times. Surveys conducted between the mid-1950s and the early 1970s show a striking change: throughout the entire population—including people of different ages, classes, and even religions—the proportion believing that "divorce is always wrong" declined precipitously and acceptance of separation and divorce increased dramatically. By now social scientists acknowledge that the stigma surrounding divorce has largely disappeared. A 2008 Gallup poll showed that nearly three-quarters of Americans found divorce to be a "morally acceptable option."

I asked the experts, "If a young couple came to you and was thinking of calling it quits, what kind of advice would you give?" They strongly recommended that people buck the contemporary casual attitude and view marriage as an unbreakable, lifelong commitment. There are of course qualifications: no one believed that a person should stay in a mentally or physically abusive relationship, one marked by repeated infidelity, or a situation of extreme and irresolvable conflict.

They do believe, however, that most marriages do not end for those reasons. They are more often terminated because one partner feels that his or her needs are not being met, because of "falling out of love," or because of routine disagreements about minor issues. The experts hold that such issues can be surmounted but that couples only have the will to do so if they believe that they *must* stay and work on the marriage.

From their standpoint at the end of a married life, the experts base this lesson not on moral grounds so much as on their own experience of problems and finding ways to resolve them in marriage. Most of the experts' marriages have been difficult for periods of time. By struggling through those periods—because they believed they did not have the option of walking out—they emerged with compromises, renewed relationships, and often the reward of a fulfilling, intact marriage in later life.

There's one key difference between the experts' view of marriage and that of many couples today: they believe that a marriage is not simply "two people who love one another." They share a commitment to the institution of marriage as good in and of itself and to the belief that a vow to stay together "for better or for worse" actually binds you to that statement. Rather than view marriage as a voluntary partnership that lasts as long as the passion does, the experts see it as a profound cultural arrangement that we should respect, even if things go sour over the short term.

Based on her fifty-four years of marriage, Amelia Callender, seventy-six, provides an example of the belief that faithfulness to marriage itself is crucial.

LOOK BEYOND THE PASSION of the moment. Realize that it's a commitment that you're making for life. There will be rough spots and there will be times of being mad at each other. But that's okay. I'm sure that each of us felt at times, "This is not worth it." But we knew it was. We made a commitment to the vows of marriage. A commitment to our children, and now to our grandchildren, because we want to be examples for all of them. In committing to marriage itself, you're saying, "We've shared so many good times, so many troubled times, and that's all part of and woven into our lives. We wouldn't trade that for anything."

Let's return to Mark Minton, one of the most reflective experts on the issue of marriage. He makes the point that all of life necessarily involves struggle, and if it doesn't, we aren't fully living. His approach to marriage takes into account that all long relationships involve both joy and struggle, and it is based on an understanding that a commitment to stay in a relationship can have enormous payoffs.

THERE WERE TIMES WHEN we really had a hard time with each other. But a marriage deserves to be worked at enough to get it to a better place. It takes a stubborn hopefulness, a stubborn commitment that you take seriously. You hang in there, work at it, and over time you realize that persistence pays off. Any relationship will go through dark times as well as bright times, so that the high points are richly enjoyed, but there are going to be valleys that you are going to have to track through and not give up. Quitting working on the relationship means giving up on all the future possibilities. Look, it will be struggle, but it has to be struggle or else it's not a fully lived life.

A surprising number of experts related how they reached a turning point in their marriage when they nearly abandoned it but at the critical moment decided to turn back. As a result of that decision, they reaped many years of happy married life and are grateful that they did not end the relationship.

Sandy Hudgens, eighty-nine, was married during World War II, right before her husband went overseas. Their daughter was born while her husband was fighting, and the first time he saw her was when she was one and a half years old. Married life was very difficult after his return.

HE WAS IN PATTON'S army in the Battle of the Bulge— serious combat. When he came home, he was a different person. It was a very difficult thing to see. He was suffering from battle fatigue. He never changed back to how I knew him. He had been lighthearted before, singing and happy, and when he came home, not at all. He would get up in the middle of the night and walk through the neighborhood. He had horrible dreams. He had a tough time. So we had to adjust a lot.

But I want to tell you something about turning points. When my husband got back from overseas, he was drinking. Some men in the service that came back from World War II started drinking just to not think about it. He never was a nasty drinker or stumbling or falling, nothing like that. But we had a series of bad things that happened, and one night he sat down and began to drink very heavily. I never saw him do that before. And it got to the point where he wasn't nice, and so I went over to him and I said, "I have to tell you. You need to stop drinking or I'm going to leave."

I didn't know where I was going to go or what I was going to do, but I knew I would survive if I had to. And he did it—he stopped drinking. And I made the decision to stay in the marriage, although I could have left. I was very close to doing so.

Sandy is immensely grateful that she did not leave the marriage and believes that others should stay the course and keep trying to improve the relationship:

> BUT THE SAD PART is, too many young people now are giving up too early, too soon. They'll say, "I don't need this. I'm going to get a divorce." We didn't do that. In our day we stuck with it. Divorce was not in our language. We tried. We kept at it and we tried. He lived for twenty more years, and the two of us—it was wonderful. It was a great life. It was like a bonus for him and for me.

Postscript:
Don't Go to Bed Angry

There's an underlying coherence to what the experts tell us about marriage. They warn us that a long-term marriage can be difficult, that it's not always a picnic, and that it has many ups and downs. These challenges will confront even the strongest and happiest marriage. Each of the lessons in this chapter represents a way of *making marriage easier.* Here's the "refrigerator list" of lessons for successful married life:

1. **Marry someone a lot like you.** Similarity in core values and background is the key to a happy marriage. And forget about changing someone after marriage.

2. **Friendship is as important as romantic love.** Heart-thumping passion has to undergo a metamorphosis in lifelong relationships. Marry someone for whom you feel deep friendship as well as love.

3. **Don't keep score.** Don't take the attitude that marriage must always be a fifty-fifty proposition; you can't get out exactly what you put in. The key to success is having both partners try to give more than they get out of the relationship.

4. **Talk to each other.** Marriage to the strong, silent type can be deadly to a relationship. Long-term married partners are talkers (at least to one another, and about things that count).

5. **Don't just commit to your partner—commit to marriage itself.** Make a commitment to the idea of marriage and take it seriously. There are enormous benefits to seeing the marriage as bigger than the immediate needs of each partner.

There's one saying many of the experts used that goes to the heart of these lessons. I came to expect it when I asked for their advice about how to have a long and happy marriage. It might come at the beginning; it might come at the end. It wasn't usually the main point and often it popped up as an afterthought: "Oh and of course I should add . . ." But if there was one ubiquitous recommendation about marriage it was this: "Don't go to bed angry."

Why, of all the things we can do to keep a marriage strong, is it so important to make sure anger is put to bed before we are? As I began to look over my own experience, I had to admit that, yes, there might be a special problem about going to sleep while still stewing over a marital argument. Although one can muster the energy (and sometimes the perverse satisfaction) to spar and quarrel throughout an entire day, there is indeed *something* about experiencing disappointment, resentment, even fury in the most intimate of spaces. It just feels wrong. The end of the day means that very soon someone is going to have the last word, and someone will be deeply hurt, and there will be nowhere further along the road to travel.

The experts are telling us something profound: namely, most things that couples disagree upon aren't worth more than a day's combat. Feel the pressure of the close of the day and let it push you toward a resolution whether you feel ready or not. Perhaps you can decide for whom the issue is most important and allow that person to win. Let your feeling out in a letter that is never sent. Establish that the issue is really "small stuff" and let it go. Accept that there is a serious issue that needs to be dealt with, and at the end of the day agree on a plan for future discussion. Whatever can be done, do it before the lights go out.

The old know this lesson, but the young must take it seriously too. Wilma Yager, seventy-five, opened up my understanding when she said:

> NEVER GO TO BED without saying "I love you." I don't care if you have to grind your teeth and say, "I love you." But you do it. You've got to do it. You never know what's going to happen during the night.

"You never know what's going to happen during the night." That statement is something elders know in their hearts, and we should too. The night, when we are unconscious, is an uncertain time; who knows what will happen? The joy that many of the experts express on waking in the morning next to a partner of decades is the flip side of this insight. Each additional day together is a gift. The end of the day means the end of hostilities, the recognition that the underlying shared values and commitment to the relationship trump the need for one last dig or self-righteous justification. Because the end of the day could, of course, be the end.

CHAPTER 3

❖ ❖ ❖

Glad to Get Up in the Morning

Lessons for a Successful and Fulfilling Career

Jerry DeVries, 78

BY THE TIME I was a teenager, I was working on the farm seven days a week when I wasn't in school, and many days before school and after school. I was a teenager and getting up at four in the morning to milk the cows and feed the cattle, and then going to school at seven thirty, getting out of school at three thirty in the afternoon, and then getting on the school bus and then going back out to the farm and working until after dark. And that's before you even started

studying. I knew what hard work was, and when you're fifteen or sixteen that's a pretty good lesson.

IN ONE OF THE earliest formulations we know of, work is portrayed as a punishment. After eating from the tree of the knowledge of good and evil, Adam and Eve are forced out of (presumably
work-free) paradise into what we might now call the real world.
God's parting remarks include, "By the sweat of your brow you will
eat your food until you return to the ground" (Genesis 3:19). No
more leisurely walks in the garden in the cool of the day, no more
plucking fruit whenever hunger strikes. Adam, Eve, and their children were sentenced to lifetimes of hard work.

Proposed utopias notwithstanding, no one has come up with
a system by which humans can avoid working. On a fundamental
level, we work to survive—to obtain the food, clothing, and shelter
we need. Jobs vary from being a business magnate in Mumbai to a
street cleaner in Manhattan, but the basic principle is the same: we
exchange hours of lifetime for money, and we use that money to
live. For most people, however, work means much more. It is a
primary source of meaning and purpose in life, the way we gain a
sense of self-worth and achievement, and a means of making connections with others. It is also a component of our core identity, of
the people we consider ourselves to be.

Work (and preparation for work) occupies Americans' lives for
six or more decades. And Americans work *a lot*. One sign of our
workaholic culture: in a given year, around 574 million vacation
days go unused: That equals over fifty-five hundred working lifetimes in a single year. Each year the average worker spends over
eighteen hundred hours on the job and sometimes longer, working
extra shifts or at a second job to make ends meet.

In contemporary society, we are much less likely than past
generations to stay in one job for an entire career. Young adults

entering the labor force will change jobs five or more times over the course of their lives. Finding enjoyable and meaningful work has become a challenge for many Americans, and not just for people starting out. Dissatisfied or burned-out workers are looking for midcareer changes and the newly retired are angling for what have come to be called "encore careers."

Sigmund Freud famously offered the opinion that love and work are the cornerstones of human happiness. In the previous chapter, we looked at what the experts had to say about love, so let's turn now to work. Tallied up, the experts have around fifty thousand years of work experience among them. They have done nearly every job you can imagine, from carhop to restaurant owner, from enlisted man or woman to commanding officer, from factory worker to factory owner. There are athletes and coaches, clergymen and clergywomen, farmers, miners, teachers, all kinds of tradespeople, corporate CEOs, retail clerks, artists, writers, actors. The entire spectrum of the American work force across the last century is represented in their ranks.

Just as their occupations varied widely, so did the career paths of the experts. Some of them diligently pursued a single career, working for decades in the same field. Others moved from job to job or among different careers (indeed, some experts believe this is the ideal career strategy). Still others had alternating spells of employment and unemployment, including women who took time out to raise children. There are experts who chose lifelong part-time work, living within financial limitations so as to be able to pursue artistic or political activities on the side. Some experts loved their work, some slogged it out in jobs they didn't really care for, and still others discovered occupational happiness late in life. From this diversity, five lessons for finding meaningful work and having a fulfilling career emerged.

The First Lesson:
Choose a Career for the Intrinsic Rewards,
Not the Financial Ones

After listening to a thousand of America's elders give advice about fulfillment at work, nothing makes me cringe more than when I hear a young person describe his or her primary goal in life as "making a lot of money." As a professor, my students say with sad regularity, "Well, I'd really like to study philosophy, but I'm good at the business courses, so I guess I should stay with that," or "I love to cook, but you can't make money doing that, so I'm premed." Many bright young people who would make wonderful teachers, social workers, or artists are seduced by the salaries and bonuses of the financial industry. By the time they finish college, they are on a career trajectory that takes on a life of its own. Once ensconced in a field—especially one that pays well—it can require heroic effort to take the dramatic step of shifting gears. And so the years go by.

The experts have a real problem with this scenario. The view from the end of the life span is straightforward: *time well and enjoyably spent trumps money anytime.* They know what it means to make a living, and they are not suggesting that we all become starving artists. But they also know firsthand that most people who decide on a profession because of the material rewards at some point look back and gasp, "What have I done?" In their view, we all need a salary to live on. But the experts concur that it's vastly preferable to take home less in your paycheck and enjoy what you are doing rather than live for the weekends and your three weeks (if you get that much) vacation a year. If doing what you love requires living with less, for the experts that's a no-brainer.

Willie Bradfield, eighty-three, is healthy and vigorous, which one might expect from a man who has devoted his life to athletics.

His career advice may come from the world of sports, but it applies to any field:

> WELL, I PLAYED FOOTBALL, basketball, and baseball in high school and went to university on an athletic scholarship. I coached at a number of different schools after that, winding up as a coach and director of recruiting at a university. I spent about thirty years at, I guess, five different schools. It was a labor of love. I didn't do it for money.
>
> That's one of the biggest things I could tell young people—to get into something that you love, that you have an aptitude for, and where you're totally happy. Because I think striving just to make money shouldn't be number one. I ended up making very little money—you would not believe what I made after thirty years of coaching. I think the most important thing is to be involved in a profession that you absolutely love, and that you look forward to going to work to every day.

Esther Brookshire, seventy-seven, worked at a number of interesting jobs and spent the last twenty years of her career directing a large volunteer program. This position was enormously fulfilling because it was in line with her personal values. Esther had the kinds of skills that would have allowed her to succeed in professions where she would have made much more money. However, she offered this advice:

> MY GRANDDAUGHTERS SAY, "OH, I've got to make this much money, and it's important for me to have money and everything." And I've said to them, "Just make sure that what you're doing to get that money makes you happy. Be-

cause the job can pay a million dollars a week, but if you're not happy, you're never going to enjoy it. And it's for life. Remember, you have to get up in the morning and do it every day." My recommendation would be to make sure that if you are searching for a purpose, it includes others. Then the self will take care of itself.

Another recommendation has to do with balancing money and time. If you are willing to accept a lower income level, you can gain enormous benefits by choosing part-time work as a lifestyle. Imagine if you suddenly had more leisure than work time. Some experts made this decision: living on much less money, renting rather than owning a house, and forgoing expensive consumer goods to pursue a job and a lifestyle they enjoy.

Kevin Tetreault is still working well into his sixties. He loves his job as a manager at a local soup kitchen. At this point in his life, he's found "the best job I've ever had. It's a job with people and I like working with people. It's a job that is outside of the profit-making world, so there isn't that kind of pressure and stress." A key to his work satisfaction is forgoing full-time employment:

> FOR MANY YEARS I'VE worked part time, and that's really important for me and I would recommend it for everybody. I don't get so worn out or burned out. I've done other things in the past, like teaching, but working part time allows me the freedom to do other things I'm interested in. The job does put constraints on the money I can make, but I have enough money to live the way I want to live, and having a lot more is not an issue. If people can try not to worry about money and have time to volunteer and do other things like that—well, it's kind of like that book title, do what you love and the money will follow.

Psychologists have a term for this worldview: they use the word "eudaimonia" (from the Greek) to describe happiness derived from activities that are rewarding in and of themselves. This is contrasted with "hedonia"—as in hedonism. People with hedonic motivations look at work primarily as a way to acquire material possessions. In contrast, eudaimonic individuals who are motivated by goals that emphasize personal growth, contributing to the community, and meaningful relationships are typically much happier at work.

In this book I have mostly avoided statistical analyses. But I would like to throw this quantitative finding at you. Looking at the data on this lesson, one of the most striking points is what the thousand-plus experts *didn't* say. When asked about their prescription for happiness at work, what wasn't mentioned spoke the loudest. And fancy statistics aren't necessary because the results are so clear.

No one—not a single person out of a thousand—said that to be happy you should try to work as hard as you can to make money to buy the things you want.

No one—not a single person—said it's important to be at least as wealthy as the people around you, and if you have more than they do it's real success.

No one—not a single person—said you should choose your work based on your desired future earning power.

Now it may sound absurdly obvious when worded in this way. But this is in fact how many people operate on a day-to-day basis. The experts did not say these things; indeed almost no one said anything remotely like them. Instead they consistently urged finding a way to earn enough to live on without condemning yourself to a job you dislike. Joyce Casias, seventy-nine, offered this insight:

THERE WILL ALWAYS BE many who are richer or more distinguished than I am, so if my purpose in working is to attain these extrinsic rewards, I will be disappointed, for I will always compare myself to those whose attainments are greater. But if I work principally for the pleasure or the fulfillment it gives me, my success is assured. There are few blessings greater than finding such work and keeping it.

The advice from the experts is clear: if there's another career you wish you could pursue but you are worried that it will bring a drop in income, *do it anyway*. There is literally no time to waste. No book can tell you precisely how to do this, but take the core lesson to heart. From somewhere around age twenty we begin forty or more years of working, for eight or more hours a day, forty-eight or more weeks each year. No financial reward, they tell us, can make up for the time lost on a boring, tedious job.

I will let Morgan Grandison, seventy-six, have the last word, because he articulated this lesson so well. If you are still debating whether money is more important than enjoyment of work, pin this up on your bulletin board:

A BIG PROBLEM IS that people look at how much they're making an hour. But I tell them, "If you're not happy, get out." Because I don't care how much money you're making, if you go to work in the morning and say, "Oh jeez, I hate this job—I wish I could get out," well, get out! You just keep your eyes and ears open until you say, "Now, there's something I would be interested in." Then you say to yourself, "But I'm going to be losing five dollars an hour." So you talk to your significant other about it: "Okay, I'm going to be losing two hundred dollars a week, but I'm going to be a lot happier, and a lot easier to get along with, and we can still make ends meet." There are an awful lot of unhappy people out there who have been hog-tied to jobs they hated. They kept them only because of the dollars and cents, and not because of life.

The Second Lesson:
Don't Give Up on Looking for a Job That Makes You Happy

The experts understand that you may not hit that job you love on the first (or second) try; many have experienced wrong turns themselves. But they urge you not to fumble along in the inertia of a job you dislike. They have told us that people take a wrong turn in choosing a job based on salary alone. They do not think we should be pushed into a career by parents or peers. But if these things happen, the tragedy isn't finding ourselves in the wrong job; it's staying there.

Carolyn Tafoya, seventy-eight, presents this life lesson well. She tried a few dead ends before finding her life's work in health education, helping people learn to live with chronic illness.

> I THINK IT'S EXTREMELY important to get your goals set on a job that you really enjoy doing. It makes all the difference in the world if you have to do nine to five every day in something that you dislike. Perhaps you can't originally get that kind of a position, even though your education was directed in that area, but don't stay in a job you dislike just because you need the money. Keep your goals set toward a position where you enjoy going to work every day. You need to find a job situation that you really like. Look at it in terms

of a long time, because you will be working thirty years or more.

Gerald Hendrix, whose advice you may remember from the last chapter, became a work and career guru for me. He's a retired New York City entrepreneur who succeeded (and, he will tell you, failed as well) in a number of different businesses. But ultimately he came out on top, parlaying a large company, real estate holdings, and other enterprises into a career that was both economically and personally rewarding. He remains as active at eighty-two as when he was working, serving on boards of charitable organizations and mentoring younger businesspeople.

Gerald's recommendation for managing your career trajectory when starting out was unexpected and extremely useful. "Divide your work life into manageable chunks that you can afford to spare." Gerald is a poker player and he likes gambling analogies. "In this case you can afford to risk a year, maybe two or even three on a job that isn't immediately satisfying. The bet is worth the risk. But don't spend any more time at it than it takes to know if it's right for you." He continued:

HERE'S WHAT I BELIEVE people should do. Whatever field they want to go into, I would spend a few years in the field working for somebody. Take a learner's standpoint, to learn as much about the field and know that it's the field they want. And if that's not the field, then within a year or two go on. You made a mistake—go try something else.

It's the time limit and the awareness that you can change course that allow the freedom to experiment and take risks.

DON'T BE AFRAID TO move around and try different things, no matter how old you are. The most important thing you want to find out is who you are and what capabilities you have. Give yourself a time limit to dig into yourself and find out what you need. In this period there's no way around it, you have to be a risk taker. Because if you don't take any risks, you don't get any sweetness out of life. And the truth of the matter is that the sweetness in life comes with the risk. It doesn't come with playing four aces in a poker hand. And I've lived my life taking risks and I wish I could tell you they were all successful, but they weren't. But you want to know something? I learned more from my failures than I did from my successes.

Of course, the struggle to find the right career can sometimes seem overwhelming. It's easy to say "Don't be afraid to search for the right career," but for many people negotiating work life means overcoming major challenges. We all need inspiration from time to time, and my regret is that I don't have room to tell the story of every expert who managed to achieve a dream job after years of trying. But there's one example of persistence and eventual success that demands sharing. Think your career path was difficult? Then listen to Martin Sanderson's story.

Martin had to fight to find the work he loved, at the cost of tremendous effort. The struggle and the rewards of his eighty-nine years are encapsulated in the first words of his interview: "I was one of the original Tuskegee Airmen."

In the early 1940s the military was almost completely segregated and the air force did not allow blacks to enlist. But what if, as a young black man, your dream in life was to fly and to serve your country? The Tuskegee Airmen came along, showing how people can accomplish the seemingly impossible if they have the will to do so. The airmen became the first African American aviators in the U.S. military and, despite unremitting discrimination, flew their missions with great heroism, destroyed German planes, and garnered a slew of medals. The Tuskegee Airmen struck a massive blow to the forces of segregation and racial prejudice in the armed forces.

To get there, Martin had to overcome the almost insurmountable odds produced by racism and discrimination:

BACK WHEN I WANTED to get into the military, before America got into the fighting in World War II, I wanted to fly an airplane. I had never been in an airplane in my life, though we'd seen them fly over. I think Lindbergh's flight across the Atlantic Ocean is what kind of stimulated me to want to do that. Well, I was a Depression-era child and pennies were very hard to come by, but I would save my pennies, go to the hobby shop, and make model airplanes because I wanted to fly so much.

Sometime in early 1941, I wanted to enlist as a pilot to fight for my country. The letter of rejection that I received said point-blank, no easy words to smooth it over, that there were no facilities to train Negroes to fly in any branch of the American military service. That ticked me off. I balled the letter up and threw it away. And I was not the only one. There were Negroes that wanted to fly—all over the United States there were others in similar situations. I went back to my job as a bellhop.

When I heard that they were going to open a school to train Negroes to fly, I applied the second time and I was rejected again. Well, I continued in my job as bellhop, and then I heard that they had dropped some of the restrictions. I applied again and I was very lucky. I passed and I continued to pass all of the examinations that I was given, and I was in the twenty-seventh class of Negroes that graduated.

Martin needed a mix of courage, drive, and forbearance to succeed in the military of the 1940s, where blacks were unusual and black officers an exotic curiosity.

> THE MILITARY WAS STRICTLY segregated. I was with this black bunch, and there was no way of getting out of the black bunch. We were an oddity. Many had never seen black officers and very, very few had seen black pilots. World War II was a real stinker for segregation. There was no integration of the unit. They did not want black officers giving white enlisted personnel orders.

Nevertheless, he achieved his dream of fighting for his country, putting his life at risk in the war in Europe:

> I WAS IN COMBAT. I'm a combat survivor. One of the questions a youth asked me was, "Were you afraid?" And I said, "Yes, I was afraid! When you let somebody get behind you who's shooting at you and they're trying to kill you and you know they are trying to kill you, you'd be afraid too if you had any sense." So I will not lie. I told him, "Yes, I was afraid." I could see the bullets coming.

Where others might have given up, Martin refused to become discouraged by the racial environment in the air force. Instead he used the military experience, despite its difficulties, to create a career path that would have been almost unimaginable to him as a child. Martin might be looking back on a lifetime as a hotel bellhop rather than as one of the pioneers of desegregation in the military, who is sought after in his ninth decade as a speaker and a living symbol of perseverance in the face of adversity. As he sums it up:

> I ACCEPT MY FELLOW man as an individual. I try not to prejudge. I try to enter any situation with an open mind. I don't let being colored keep me from doing something. I'm very proud of the life I've lived. I'm proud of having been a black pilot and of my contribution to society. My legacy—I don't know just what it's going to be. I haven't written it yet. But I do hope that I've contributed something to mankind, individually as well as collectively.

The point of these examples is that many people in the experts' generation were saddled with dead-end jobs—that's the kind of economy they grew up in (and it was a lot worse than ours is today). Based on that experience, they believe that we should never stop searching for a fulfilling career. It may take years, but we should never give up if we're unhappy on the job—we spend too much of our short lifetimes working to remain stuck in jobs we hate.

The Third Lesson:
Make the Most of a Bad Job

"Find something you love to do and do it." "Nothing is worse than dragging yourself every day to a job you dislike." "If you don't like your job, get out of it." That is the essence of the experts' advice, but I bet you can see the one flaw in it: we can't, realistically, always be in jobs we love. Indeed most of us have had at least one job, or a string of jobs, we've hated.

Mine was as a dishwasher in the now defunct Bit o' Glouces-ter Restaurant in Cambridge, Massachusetts. Located in a Holiday Inn and profusely decorated in a faux-nautical theme (think fish-nets and buoys hanging on the walls), it served mediocre food in a soulless hotel environment. My job was to wash unending sinkfuls of dishes and pots and to bus tables, for which the waitresses grudg-ingly shared their tips. Minutes dragged by like hours. I remember actually feeling grateful one day when I cut my hand on a steak knife—I needed stitches, but at least I got to go home early!

Many of us find ourselves in jobs that, even if not so extreme, are less than ideal: starter jobs, work that's the best available where we live, entry-level jobs in a field in which we hope someday to make a career or in a workplace environment that we find stuffy, unpleasant, or stagnating. We see people every day who don't seem to be having much fun: droopy-eyed store clerks, irritable bank tellers, bored fast-food workers. People in those situations may be tempted to say, "Take all that 'love your job' stuff and shove it!"

I found that whenever I encountered a conundrum like this, the experts provided an answer. One way to sum up the expert viewpoint would be to modify the Stephen Stills song lyric "And if you can't be with the one you love, honey, love the one you're with." Okay, modify it pretty heavily to something like "And if you can't have the job you love, honey, find something worthwhile about the one you're in." Let us recall that the experts have probably had more experience than you have in tedious, boring, unpleasant jobs; few of them followed the contemporary pathway of moving from school and leisure-time activities to college and then to a white-collar job. The most successful among them learned how to take the most mundane and dreary job and transform it into a learning experience.

One of my expert guides in this lesson was Sam Winston, eighty-one. Sam held a number of high-level jobs throughout his career. He trained as an engineer but also worked in marketing and as a general manager. He attributes his considerable career success specifically to his ability to learn from jobs he *didn't* like. The key is to see them as learning experiences and to take advantage of any opportunity to gather knowledge about an industry or occupation.

> ONE IMPORTANT THING FOR young people is to be observant. No matter what the task is, whether you like it or not, it's very important to learn everything you can about what's happening around you. You never know when that may be of great value later. I've had many different experiences throughout my life where I really didn't like what I had to do and I would feel what I was doing was inconsequential. But the lessons I learned doing those things played an important part in my life. For example, I had to work my way through college, in many what you may consider meaningless jobs. Later on they were very valuable for me as an employer, to help me understand my people. I would tell younger people that no matter what the experience is—*learn*. See what's happening.

Sam provided another highly useful insight: We don't just learn from the best and the brightest; we also learn from the duds and the toxic colleagues.

> PEOPLE ARE VERY IMPORTANT. I have a saying that "There is some good in everyone." But there is an important corollary to that. If nothing else, you can always say, "There's a bad example." There's a quote for you. That's not to say people aren't any good. The thing is that most people are good. But the corollary is, even if you don't think they are, they can always serve as a bad example for you. You can

learn from everyone, no matter who it is. No matter what their status, you can learn from them.

How to make this happen? Stephanie Farrington, seventy-five, was forced to drop out of college for financial reasons and hit the streets looking for work, eventually winding up in a bank. An outsider looking at her job might have seen it as both routine and stressful, offering little opportunity or fulfillment. But Stephanie saw it differently and turned the job into a deeply meaningful opportunity to serve others:

THE BANK WAS HIRING, so I got a job there for supposedly two years and I never got back to college, and that is a regret in many ways. I was in the credit department, and I supervised the collection of loans. I came to see it as being like caregiving. Because I found that the people who were not paying, 90 percent of the time it was because of catastrophic things. For most of the people, I took it as caregiving, because you couldn't demand they get six payments in all at once. You worked with them—you helped them make the payments. You got to know them, and they were good people. And when they got on their feet, you wanted their business downstairs in the bank again.

My boss used to say to me, "You know, I don't understand it. I go to a meeting upstairs and the bank president gives me a letter praising my employees in the collection department. They're not supposed to like us!" But they did, because we found a way to help them.

Another tactic recommended by the experts is to salvage a less-than-ideal job by becoming really good at it. A disinterested attitude compounds the boredom and ennui one feels in such a position; the attitude of mastering and even improving the job is an antidote. Antoinette Watkins worked in bookkeeping and accounting, later becoming a departmental administrator for a university. "I had a job I loved. I just loved my last job." But earlier jobs she held were much further from ideal. Here's how she coped:

> EVEN IF YOUR JOB is not the ultimate and it's not the most exciting—do it well, because you feel so much better personally if you've done a good job. There's something about just wasting time at a job that I don't understand. So learn what you can, use what you can from it. You can learn from any job, and that's what you need to do.

This lesson doesn't apply just to white-collar jobs. George Villalba, seventy-nine, never finished high school but was very satisfied with his work life. When asked for his advice, he focused on one reason for making the most of any job: you will feel better about yourself.

> THERE WAS THIS ONE guy, and everyone seemed to like my welding better than his for one simple reason: I don't care how good you are at welding, but you take pride in whatever you do. It doesn't matter what job you do—do the very best you can and be proud of what you've done. He would weld as well as I did, but he would never go to the extreme to make it look good.

On occasion I would find an expert who could sum up a lesson perfectly. Keith Koon, whose wisdom about married life we heard in the last chapter, did this for the idea that you should make the most even of a bad job. Keith was a management consultant, improving organizational culture and motivating employees. Based on that experience, his solution is to milk any job for what you can learn:

> WHAT ABOUT WHEN YOU are in a job you find hard to do? How can you benefit from it? Be aware of every opportunity there is for learning. Be aware, know what is happening. The goal in the job is to continually learn. No matter what job we have, we will learn something that we will use later in life. So a lot of people would say, "Well, Keith, this job is so boring. I'm not learning anything." They've got to find the learning. Always look for opportunities within the job you're doing, and accumulate knowledge. What have you learned from this lousy job? Don't just blow it off. Consciously work at it because then you'll use that knowledge. Believe that it's the learning experience you need at that time.

The Fourth Lesson:
Emotional Intelligence Trumps Every Other Kind

Although I do consulting for businesses and government, I've spent most of my life in academia, working with fellow scientists. Academia is considered to be one of the true meritocracies, where scientifically proficient workaholics can have fantastic success despite an inability to negotiate interpersonal relations. But is this really the case? Not in my experience.

I once had a colleague who seemed to have it made. He was energetic and hardworking. He had a nearly encyclopedic knowledge of his research area. He published in top scientific journals and was awarded major grants from prestigious funding agencies. At one point he decided to improve his position at the university by soliciting a competing job offer. He went to the dean of the college and asked for a counteroffer, including a larger salary. The dean asked the faculty in the department for their approval. To my colleague's great surprise, the faculty voted almost unanimously against it and he was forced to take the other job, which he didn't really want.

The reason? No one could get along with him. He had been rude to colleagues, engaging in petty disputes over minor issues and acting in a superior and condescending way toward everyone with whom he crossed paths. In the end people cared less about his technical expertise and achievements than they did about his lack of interpersonal skills. Even in a world where objective achievement is supposed to rule, the inability to get along with others can trump professional accomplishments.

The experts, you will recall, come from hundreds of different occupations and employers. They have observed people who succeed at work and those who crash and burn. It is on such experiences that this lesson is based. Their consensus: no matter how talented you are, no matter how brilliant—*you must have interpersonal skills to succeed.* Many young people today are so focused on gaining technical expertise that they lose sight of this key to job success: traits like empathy, consideration, listening skills, and the ability to resolve conflicts are fundamentals in the workplace.

Sonny Lee, seventy-two, an engineer, highlighted the importance of interpersonal skills on the job. Like many of the successful experts, he focused on the need to develop empathy in the workplace toward subordinates, coworkers, and, yes, even bosses.

ONE THING IS THE same, no matter what work you do: you will be doing it with other people. Your technical ability in your job is important, but how you work and get along with other people is important too. I think most of us end up, one way or another, in the people-pleasing business. I would stress the importance of not only knowing your field and your area of interest, but also knowing why other people don't act and believe the same way you do. And I know a lot of times in my work it was frustrating that not everybody saw things the way I did. And yet I've finally learned that it's more important to get along with one another than to persuade them, probably against their will, to believe what I do.

The experts maintain that empathy at work can be learned. Shelley Donaldson, sixty-seven, a former human service agency director, recommends that conscious effort be exerted to understand the perspectives of others:

> I CERTAINLY KNOW THAT I don't know everything, but I have learned how to ask better questions. You have to understand every issue from somebody else's perspective. I used to make my leadership team debate an issue from the perspective that they disagreed with because they often only looked at it from one perspective. You have to see it from both sides.

Larry Tice, eighty-six, learned about the importance of interpersonal skills and empathy for coworkers through military service. Many of the experts who served in World War II or in the Korean War came from small, homogeneous communities and few had traveled much. They found themselves suddenly thrown together with a dizzyingly diverse array of people from different parts of the country and, depending on where they were stationed, the world. Larry described his experience serving in the Second World War:

WHEN I WENT INTO the service, I was a young boy from Vermont. A little hick town. And I lived on the right side of the tracks, okay? My whole family was well known throughout town, well respected and everything. I got into the navy and I was just another punk. And I learned how to get along with people. That was the biggest lesson and one that has helped me all through life. Because you're cramped in, living aboard ship, and you've got to get along with people because you have no choice. And these are people that you never saw before. I've learned to accept people until they give me a reason not to. I don't care who you are, what you are, how you are—you're fine with me until you prove the opposite. That's what you need at work: to be sociable and to get along with the people you are working with.

We've heard from the worlds of business and technology, but Tim Burke comes from a very different work environment. We live in a time of occupational mobility, in which people seem to cross the country on a whim for a new job. Not so for Tim. He summed up his life like this:

I'M EIGHTY-SEVEN YEARS OLD, and I am the seventh-generation patriarch of my family farm. It was established by my great-great-great-great grandfather in 1798, which puts me in a position where we are in the second decade of our third century. This is a family farm, but we've had up-wards of thirty-five people in the business because we had cows for milk and processed it right here on the farm. In my case, you might say I was born to do what I did. It didn't occur to me to do something else.

Managing a large farming operation—one that had not just financial but also great personal significance—provided a hands-on education in managing employees. Tim highlighted understanding employees as individuals, reserving judgment about mistakes, and, above all, having empathy.

> DEAL WITH EACH EMPLOYEE with patience. Don't rush to judgment, and remember that you are not living their lives. There may be a lot of things I would like to criticize about my workers. But I don't. I tell myself, "Tim, you are not there." I don't make judgments on people or scold them, because I haven't walked a mile or lived a day in their shoes. Things look very different to the outsider.
>
> I had three or four individuals that knew more than I did about their work but grew up under different conditions than I did. I didn't try to run the work that they were supposed to be doing, because they knew more about it. I would consult with them—how come this or how come that?—but I was careful not to get in there and throw my weight around.

As I immersed myself in the experts' views on work, I uncovered one underlying principle behind their emphasis on interpersonal skills: *maintaining a healthy humility*. Many elders said that we must respect the knowledge of other workers and in particular those who are lower in the hierarchy. They reject the image of leadership emanating from an overseeing boss who knows best, suggesting instead a willingness to learn from everyone in the workplace.

Anthony Scheel, seventy-three, worked as an engineer at a number of major corporations as well as in his own consulting business. Anthony attributes his success to one basic principle: take yourself down a peg (or two). At one point in his career, he was thrown in with 150 other employees in an exciting, intense environment. Anthony spent his life working in highly technical fields—the kinds that make people, when you start talking about your job, stare uncomprehendingly until their eyelids begin to flutter. Nevertheless, he found that it was the people skills that counted and in particular a sense of humility:

> WELL, I THINK I had the attitude that I might have certain skills but mostly everybody here knows more than I do. And that if I'm going to add value, it's going to be by making use of these people or by collecting information from them or marshaling what it is they're doing. This means that whatever they give me to do I'm going to try to do it to the best of my ability, working with whomever I have to work with.

Father Jim Scott, seventy-seven, a Jesuit priest who has been an academic administrator for much of his career, says with a bemused shake of his head, "I've always been in charge of something, for some reason." But one reason is clear—Father Jim has been closely attuned to the interpersonal environment everywhere he has been a leader. The key for him is to focus on others rather than on himself—not just for ethical reasons but *because it works*.

> I WAS BROUGHT UP in a family where we were taught to focus, not on ourselves, but on other people. To focus outward rather than inward. I have put this to good use in my work. A young man heading off into his profession asked

me recently, "What lesson do you have for me before I go?" I said, "It's very simple. No matter whom you meet, no matter where you meet them, always presume that they're much better than you are. Presume that they're head and shoulders above you, and you'll have no problem." When I look around, the most devastating Achilles' heel that I see people suffering from is that they take themselves too seriously. While it's very important to take others seriously, don't take yourself that seriously. If you do, then you've really got a problem.

Father Jim offered a striking metaphor that has helped me in my own work life: the mirror versus the window.

IN MY WORK I'VE had to deal with some of our men who've gone through long periods of desolation. For priests this can be really overwhelming. I tell them something they have found very helpful: "Stop looking at yourself. Because when you do, you're looking at yourself in the mirror, and you know exactly what you look like. Go over to the window and look outside and see."

For someone used to being in charge, their ego can be so heavily on the line. Because people so often struggle to keep their self-esteem up and compare themselves with other people. It clouds their judgment. In that case: you're looking at yourself in the mirror and you've got to get out of it and look out the window.

Taken together, the experts' advice is to move well beyond the substance of your job and devote equal effort to learning how to maximize relationships with others at work. They recognize that, no matter how stellar your performance, you are unlikely to leap out of bed eager to go to work if your workplace relationships are negative and stressful. Further, your pathway to success will be blocked if you are unable to understand the motivations and aspirations of coworkers. A healthy humility has worked for many of the experts: respecting the knowledge of others and stepping outside of oneself—looking out the window instead of into the mirror.

The Fifth Lesson:
Everyone Needs Autonomy

Let me pose a hypothetical question. Imagine you have a well-paying office position. In that job your work is almost totally regimented. You must conduct your tasks in a rigidly scheduled fashion, accomplishing them in a precise order and on a carefully determined schedule. Your breaks are exactly timed, and you will be reprimanded if you shift your tasks or their sequencing.

Now let's take the same job but at lower pay. In this case you have to accomplish the same tasks, but you can work out the schedule yourself. As long as the work is done well and on time, you can plan your own day, take breaks when you like, even shift your schedule depending on family or other personal conflicts. If you have an idea of how to improve your job, your suggestions are welcomed and you can make the changes you believe are needed. You have, in a word, autonomy.

The dictionary tells us that "autonomy" means "the ability to act on one's own or independently" and "self-directing freedom." And that, according to the experts, is exactly what you want from your job. Given a choice between the examples I just provided, here's what they would tell you: by all means take the second of the two jobs—lower pay be damned. Based on their life experience, autonomy and flexibility are the keys to an enjoyable job, and the more freedom, the better off you are. Look for maximum autonomy in a job, and work as hard as necessary to secure it.

You can achieve greater autonomy in a number of ways, from choice of profession to working your way up to positions of greater responsibility to going into business on your own. However you do it, you will be much happier than if you stay "in the middle," as Anthony Scheel put it:

I WAS IN MIDDLE management, with a number of good colleagues. And we all got kicked around. I mean, the middle is pretty high in any company, but mostly in the middle you get kicked around. If you get to the very top, then you can deal with being in the company. I've had enough of this to know that's what happens. The middle is really a tough place to be. You're responsible for most of the jobs and you're really vulnerable.

Joe McCluskey, seventy, shared a similar experience:

LIFE'S WORK IS MORE important than lifestyle. It's what you do all day long that provides the most profound satisfaction in life. It's nice to live in pleasant circumstances, but it's no substitute for doing something you enjoy and doing it well. There's no harm in having both though. Hands-on involvement gives me the greatest satisfaction. I once spent time as a corporate manager and found it unsatisfying to be far away from operations, where the real action was. I started my own small company, made myself the COO, and found that rolling up my sleeves every morning and making things happen was the fun I'd been looking for.

It's not just high-level executives who appreciate the importance of autonomy. Betsy Glynn, eighty-three, worked her way up
to being an office manager. When asked if she liked that job, she
nodded:

> YES, I DID, MOSTLY because nobody told me what to do.
> Don't boss me. I always say that when you're an office man-
> ager you figure you know how to run the place. At least
> when you're the manager you can make things get done in
> a certain way instead of being an underling and saying,
> "Oh, now they want me to do this, and this is the stupidest
> idea." When you don't have a say in things, you could feel
> terrible. It's like: I've got this all figured out to do it this way,
> and now they tell me I can't do it. It's better to have some
> freedom in your job.

The experts who most valued autonomy in work were those
who spent much of their working life without it. Glenn Carvey
struggled financially early in his life and worked in some dead-end
jobs, but he found an autonomous and fulfilling spot toward the
end of his career. Glenn, now retired at age eighty, started his lifetime of hard work as a child.

> GROWING UP, I LOOKED ahead to a life of working be-
> cause that's what we did—the whole family worked. It was
> the Depression. Nobody had any money. Then when I was
> first married, I was working two or three jobs. I'd go to
> work from eight to five and then drive to some gas station
> and work from six to eleven My wife used to pack me two
> lunches, and I'd eat one sandwich at the first job and the
> other on the way to my second job. Then on the weekends I

would deliver phone books, whatever. We were broke. I had sixty bucks in the bank when I got married, so we made payments on our furniture in installments and by the time we paid it off it was worn out.

He eventually found work in the retail tire business, working for a large company for nearly two decades. But what that work lacked was autonomy. Finally Glenn achieved a position where, for better or worse, he was in charge. The freedom formed the capstone of his working life, allowing him to look back on his career with pleasure.

MY BEST JOB WAS the last one I had. I owned my own tire store. I was finally my own boss. I worked for that tire company, started changing tires, worked my way up to store manager, but it wasn't my own place. It's all what someone else tells you to do. But I finally got my own place and I loved it. I could do what I wanted to do. It was fun. Part of it's that when I took in some money, it was mine, you know? It didn't belong to some corporation. It was my money. By the same token, if I had a bad day, that was mine too. But I was responsible. You don't get all this when you're working for someone else.

When the experts discuss their work lives, two themes go hand in hand: purpose (beyond earning a salary) and autonomy. Neither one can be found in every job, every time, but without them work can become a miserable burden.

Postscript:
The First Thing in the Morning

The sweep of the experts' working lives is truly remarkable. My oldest interviewee, age 110, brought me to attention when she said, "My first job? I remember it well, because my first day of work was the day World War I ended." Many started with hard manual labor on farms and in factories, went on to college, and completed their careers in previously unimagined jobs in the high-tech economy. There was surprising consensus, however, on the five lessons for finding satisfying work and making the most of a career.

Here's the refrigerator list:

1. **Choose a career for the intrinsic rewards, not the financial ones.** The biggest career mistake people make is selecting a profession based only on potential earnings. A sense of purpose and passion for one's work beats a bigger paycheck any day.

2. **Don't give up on looking for a job that makes you happy.** According to the experts, persistence is the key to finding a job you love. Don't give up easily.

3. **Make the most of a bad job.** If you find yourself in a less-than-ideal work situation, don't waste the experience; many experts learned invaluable lessons from bad jobs.

4. **Emotional intelligence trumps every other kind.** Develop your interpersonal skills if you want to succeed in the workplace. Even people in the most technical professions have their careers torpedoed if they lack emotional intelligence.

5. **Everyone needs autonomy.** Career satisfaction is often dependent on how much autonomy you have on the job. Look for the freedom to make decisions and move in directions that interest you, without too much control from the top.

Because I spend part of my work life in a medical school, I find myself occasionally thinking like a doctor (a "real" doctor, not a Ph.D. like me!). My medical colleagues pride themselves on a good diagnosis—finding the one sign or symptom that clearly shows what's wrong. There were certain statements the experts made that I came to see as diagnostic. That is, they suggest that it's highly probable something is wrong. One example arose earlier when we looked at marriage; there was a diagnosis in the exhortation "Never go to bed angry."

When it comes to evaluating your career, the experts collectively arrived at this kind of diagnostic test again. You should ask yourself this: *do I wake up in the morning looking forward to work?* You may feel ambivalent about the job, have your ups and downs, and waiver about whether it's the right career for you. But when it comes down to it, how do you feel when you get up or when you are having that first cup of coffee? Are you enthusiastic? At least in a tolerable mood and looking forward to some aspect of the workday? Or are you depressed and dreading the day ahead?

The notion of waking up with a sense of dread about the coming workday is horrifying to the experts, many of whom have been through it themselves. Sally Wilson, seventy-nine, spent three decades as a first-grade teacher and loved it. Her advice?

WELL, I THINK YOU need to pay really close attention to things that you're interested in. Because I have a lot of friends who went to college and majored in things that they

thought would make a lot of money but really had no interest for them. No amount of money is worth more than having a job that you're glad to get up and go to every morning,
instead of one you dread.

Tony Furst, seventy-six, a successful CEO, echoed this sentiment:

I HAVE LEARNED MANY lessons, but there are only a few
that in the long run are meaningful and which I have tried
to pass on to my children and students. If you can't wake
up in the morning and want to go to work, you're in the
wrong job.

Our farmer-sage Albert Folsom makes the point with his
usual creativity:

IF YOU WANT TO see the sun come up, you've got to get up
in the dark. If you have a good job, you want to be there on
time and greet the day with pleasure. Enjoy what you're doing. Because it's a long day if you don't like what you're doing.
You better get another job because there's no harsher penalty
than to wake up and go to work at a job you don't like.

You know those nightmares where you are shouting a warning
but no sound comes out? Well, that's the intensity with which the
experts wanted to tell younger people that *spending years in a job
you dislike is a recipe for regret and a tragic mistake.* There was no
issue about which the experts were more adamant and forceful.
Over and over they prefaced their comments with, "If there's one
thing I want your readers to know it's . . ." From the vantage point

of looking back over long experience, wasting around two thousand hours of irretrievable lifetime each year is pure idiocy.

So take the experts' advice and look back over the past few months. Did you wake up dreading going to work? They're not saying that you have to leap out of bed raring to go, barely able to wait to get to your desk. For many people, work doesn't have that magnetic excitement (although for some of the experts it did). However, if dread, depression, or foot-dragging reluctance characterizes how you feel as you leave for work, America's elders say it's time to look inside yourself and then outside around you. It may well be time for a change.

CHAPTER 4

❖ ❖ ❖

Nobody's Perfect

Lessons for a Lifetime of Parenting

Leo Wiseman, 70

CHILDREN ARE THE GREAT equalizers. They humble the mighty. If you think you know everything, try outsmarting a two-year-old, a teenager, or most children in between. They can be angels and devils simultaneously. They can be truthful and amazingly dishonest. They can be loving one minute and, especially teenagers, incomprehensibly hateful the next. Parenting is one profession most people are totally untrained and unprepared for. Although children share our genes, they sometimes act like aliens. They are emotionally taxing and emotionally rewarding. It is these ambiguities that make raising them interesting. Children made me grow, challenged me, and changed me. My three children are as different as rock, paper, and scissors and as unpredictable. I can't imagine life without them. My advice is to have the critters and enjoy them. After all, they hopefully will be the parents of your grandchildren!

PARENTING FORMS A CENTRAL part of most people's lives, occupying two decades or more while children are dependent and living at home. The parental role doesn't end there: most Americans will spend even longer dealing with children *after* they become adults, well into their offspring's middle age (as one interviewee put it: "Sixty-seven? My *baby* is sixty-seven?"). Decades of research, as well as common experience, have shown the truth of the adage "You are only as happy as your unhappiest child." Few experiences can be as uplifting and joyous, and as challenging and disappointing, as parenting. But in their attempts to be the best parents possible, Americans today are often at a loss about where to find useful advice. Most parents feel that they are called upon to make decisions with insufficient guidance.

We now live in an age of scientific parenting in which we are supposed to seek out expert advice based on empirical research. But is that actually what happens? Not from what I see in families around me. Thousands of studies on parenting have been conducted over the past fifty years, but very little of that knowledge actually affects what modern-day parents do. The child-rearing advice that reaches parents is often contradictory and tends to change dramatically over time. It's no wonder that mothers and fathers find themselves baffled when they encounter the daily dilemmas and problems of parenting.

But what about the experience and wisdom of the older generation? My guess is that most of us have rarely sought out older people for parenting advice. Our feelings about our own parents may be too mixed to make them likely sources of suggestions, and few younger Americans have friends in the older generation whom they can consult for child-rearing tips. And yet of all the domains in which I sought lessons for successful living from the oldest Americans, how to raise children in a complex and difficult world may well be the one where their guidance is the most useful.

As you can imagine, the elders I spoke to had plentiful tips for successful child rearing. Some of these were along the lines of parental micromanaging: teach them table manners, encourage them to learn calculus, make sure they play outside every day, get them to brush and floss, and a host of similar suggestions. On the other hand, most also offered broad guidelines for parents. This almost universal advice included to love your children, to be careful about overindulging them (especially when it comes to consumer fads), and to firmly convey your moral and ethical values.

That's all good advice, and my guess is that most parents of all ages agree with such sentiments and try their best to put them into practice (even if it's not always possible in the midst of hectic family life). But in interviewing the experts and analyzing their responses, I was looking for something different. Gently but persistently, I pushed them toward deeper lessons that went beyond platitudes. What do you know specifically, I asked, that younger parents don't? What are the key insights that can be gained only by looking back over a lifetime of parenting?

Five fundamental lessons emerged from this storehouse of parenting information. These lessons aren't guaranteed to make you a great parent, but from the experts' unique vantage point at the end of life—the top of the mountain, so to speak, surveying the long road traveled—they can help you avoid serious pitfalls. In this

chapter we'll look at lessons for parenting young children and adolescents as well as a few ideas for relating to children after they are
grown.

The First Lesson:
It's All about Time

What if out of the enormous muddle of child-rearing advice there
was a "magic bullet"? What if there was one course of action you
could take that would create loving relationships with your children, serve as an early warning system for problems they are having, and lead to a lifelong bond with them? According to the
experts, there is: *spend more time with your children*. And if necessary, *sacrifice to do it*. In our hectic and driven society, parents look
endlessly for programs, gimmicks, and therapies to improve their
relationships with their children. But our elders tell us that there is
one great contributor to lifelong closeness for which there is no
substitute: your time.

In the view of the experts, your kids don't want your money
(or what your money buys) anywhere near as much as they want
you. Specifically, they want *you with them*. Parents who work double shifts to keep the family afloat may have no choice. But if you
and your spouse work seventy-hour weeks to buy consumer goods
and take lavish vacations, you are misusing your time. Even if it
means doing with less, America's elders tell you that what you will
regret at their age is not having spent more time with your children. And it's what your children will regret too.

Over the years I've heard parents of adolescents complain that
their children don't want to spend time with them. In many of
those cases, I've noted that this isn't precisely the case. Actually, the
children don't object to spending time with their parents; it's just

that the parents want to dictate what activities they'll do together. An alternative strategy is to go along with the child's interests whether you share them or not.

I decided early on that this would be my strategy. But it was a challenge. I was raised in a family of four boys and wound up the proud father of Hannah and Sarah. Honestly, why the girls wanted to do a lot of what we did together was a mystery to me. But early on I vowed that my principle would be that if they were willing to spend time with me in an activity, I would become interested in that activity regardless of what it was. I have joked with female friends that I know more about women's shoes than any middle-aged man ought to. For years I took my daughters on trips to New York City. Other parents might have demanded force-marched visits to museums; I went to dozens of shoe stores. Also vintage clothing stores. I'd find a place to sit and listen while my daughters would ooh and aah about six-inch platform shoes or funky retro jewelry.

I found the payoff to be immense. It's not really the activity, I learned: it's the *shared time*. In off moments during whatever the activity may be, there's time to talk, to share confidences, to connect. And in those activities, the miracle of real communication sometimes occurs. I remember an essay by former treasury secretary Robert Reich about his sons. He used the analogy of a clam to emphasize that to really know our children we need to be there at exactly the right moment. Our kids are often closed up tightly like clamshells, hard on the outside but with a soft and vulnerable interior. Suddenly and unexpectedly, however, they will decide to open up, and if you're not there, Reich says, "you might as well be on the moon."

This is why time spent together is so critically important. No scheduling of "quality time" (whatever that is) will ensure that you are there at the precise moment when Matthew decides to tell you that what is *really* putting him in such a bad mood is the English teacher who just hates him, or when Allison reveals that, yes, there *is* this one boy in her Spanish class . . . The experts who missed out on spending time with their children regret it, and those who creatively manufactured time together regard it as the best decision they ever made.

Clayton Greenough, seventy-nine, has very close relationships with his son and daughter, both of whom settled nearby as adults. When asked for his lessons about child rearing, he reflected on the importance of going along with children's interests and making them shared activities.

> MAYBE IT'S AN OLD-FASHIONED way of speaking, but I feel that it's pretty important to stick with them. When my son was a sophomore in high school, I started putting up a shed in our backyard. And he was taking a shop class in high school at the time. I had him help me there, and before I knew it I'd come home from work and he'd be sitting with a toolbox, waiting to go ahead with some work. And this led him down a road where he actually saw the need for measuring and things like that and started to recognize that there is some value to arithmetic and mathematics. He eventually wound up being a mechanical designer. Now, if I hadn't been available to him at that time, I'm not sure what course he might have taken. So many of the things that he's doing now were initiated because we spent time together—the fact that there was somebody who was there and interested in what he was interested in.

The more I talked to the experts about child rearing, the clearer it became that the quality of relationships with children is directly proportional to the amount of time spent together. Interestingly, they often pointed to time shared in mundane daily activities and interactions rather than memorable "special occasions." Their message is to involve your children routinely in activities, and that requires your physical presence for large blocks of time.

Larry Handley, eighty-four, described how important such experiences were for his children:

WHEN THEY GET OLD enough to kind of help you around, you know, let them help doing things or cleaning— maybe you're out digging in the garden or something, or whatever—to share in the chores around the house or the yard. Helping either the mother or the father, doing things that are not always that easy or pleasant but, you know, to get it done. These are things that you don't realize, but they do stay with them for their whole life. They can enjoy those things and you can too.

Time spent with children is critical for another reason: it serves as a key early warning system for emerging problems. Betsy Glynn raised a son and a daughter. She was able to head off problems in their lives because she was right there with them:

IT'S SO IMPORTANT, WHILE your kids are growing up, to be with them and support them. Because otherwise you don't really have a clue what their direction is, what they like and don't like, and what they want to give their time to and what they're doing with it. This way we not only went to their games or concerts but we met the other kids on the team or in the band or whatever it was. Otherwise they would have gone off and—who knows who they would have associated with?

Let me tell you. If your kids have a concert or a game, you should put aside whatever it is—if the house needs fixing up or the laundry needs doing, it'll wait. It's more important to devote your time to whatever they're interested in. Otherwise you're going to lose them. They'll become strangers.

And in fact they can become strangers. Evidence for the importance of time spent with children also comes from those experts who were not able to do so and deeply regret it. Sarah Rothman, eighty-three, is remorseful about the excessive time her workaholic husband spent on the job and her own sacrifice of family life for work.

ENJOY YOUR CHILDREN WHILE they're young. Don't be so eager to get back to work. Because I was champing at the bit, I stayed home for five years. But instead of being so eager to get back to work, I should have enjoyed that time more and taken more time off. In the final analysis, family is the most important thing. But that lesson isn't easy to learn, and sometimes it doesn't sink in until you go to a funeral of a friend or a colleague and learn that spending time with their children made a huge difference in the lifetime of pleasure that one has.

For James Washington, eighty-three, this regret was brought home through a tragedy:

WE DID HAVE ONE sad experience. Our youngest son passed away a few years ago. He was very young. And I think it just shows you can't take life for granted, and you don't realize how short it really is, you know? It was a wake-up call as to how important family is, and it goes through your mind that you wish you'd spent more time with them because quality time is just so precious and you don't really do it as much as you should.

Elizabeth Wilson, seventy-nine, poignantly revealed her regrets about not giving more of her time and attention to her children when they were young:

THE HARDEST THING WAS that we didn't have a lot of money and I had to go back to school and to get a job. In some ways it was a good thing. But the sad thing is that you become so consumed with the job that the family becomes almost secondary. I can remember riding home with the kids in the car and being so involved in my mind, going over what had happened during the day and what I should be doing the next day, that I didn't hear those little voices and what they were sharing with one another and with me. And I have often regretted that I wasn't as much a part of that time as I could have been.

In this lesson the experts bring home three key points. First, it's your *time* that kids want, and they will look back on the hours you spend together with fondness and nostalgia. The experts remember this from their own families—indeed it is the source of most of their pleasant memories about childhood. Second, what counts the most are shared activities—time spent on hobbies, sports, camping, hunting, or fishing (it's extraordinary how many of the male experts cherish memories of hunting or fishing trips with their fathers) or in seeking out a new interest together. Third, the experts agree that we should be willing to make sacrifices to have that kind of time. If you are going to have kids, they say, it's worth it to live on less to be able to be with them.

The Second Lesson:
It's Normal to Have Favorites, but Never Show It

When you gather information from more than a thousand people, you begin to notice certain patterns. To be sure, each interview is unique—like the proverbial snowflake, no family constellation is entirely like any other. However, when interviewing people about their relationships with their children, something happens again and again, to the point that I've come to expect it more often than not.

It goes like this. In my questions about relationships with children, I eventually get to the issue of favoritism. In my first interviews it took some nerve to ask about this topic, because most parents aren't eager to discuss whether they prefer one child over another. So the first thing almost everyone says is something along these lines: "Oh no, I've always loved all my children equally!"

Then we'd talk some more. And at some point in the conversation, often the interviewee leans over, lowers her voice, and says almost conspiratorially, "But, you know, I guess there always *was* something special about Billy (or Betty) . . ."

I hate to be the one to break it to you, but *parents often have favorite children.* They really do, and if you talk to them long enough many will say so. Sometimes it's straightforward: they just like one child better than the others, and that's the way it is. More typically, parents have favorites in different domains of life. A mother will tell you that she prefers to ask Ed for advice, looks to Joan for help if she gets sick, but that she is most emotionally close to Rachel. Readers over the age of thirty-five will remember the famous Smothers Brothers routine in which Tommy complained to Dick, "Mom always liked you best!" Well, in many families this is true to some degree.

Most parents, however, deny it to their children when asked

directly. I have spent a career studying families, and I have rarely encountered a mother who when asked by one of her children, "Do you like Betty (or Billy) more than me?" answered, "Well, yes, now that you mention it, I guess I do." Our society has an overwhelmingly powerful norm of equal treatment of children and breaking that norm violates both parents' and children's sense of fairness.

In the real world, we all know that things don't always work fairly. Parents don't just experience children as their flesh and blood; they are also in human relationships with them. And when we're involved in relationships, it inevitably turns out that there are some people we like more than others—we resonate with certain individuals and see them as soul mates, whereas others don't inspire the same kind of closeness. The family is no exception. Cultural norms may tell parents that they have to distribute their love evenly, but in reality they may just, well, *like* one kid more than they do the others.

In my academic work, I have collaborated for many years with Jill Suitor, a professor at Purdue University, on studies of parental favoritism. This work includes a large-scale survey of mothers and many of their adult children. We have found that most mothers willingly identify the child they prefer (or don't prefer). For example, about 70 percent of mothers identify one child to whom they are most emotionally close and over 75 percent name a single child with whom they feel most comfortable discussing a personal problem. On the flip side, about four-fifths of mothers name one child with whom they have the most conflicts and disagreements. This kind of "within-family differentiation," as child psychologists call it, is the norm rather than the exception.

Sophie Fischer is a storehouse of information about parenting. She has five highly successful children whom she raised with her businessman husband (now deceased) in the suburbs. Both Sophie and her children report an idyllic family life in which the kids did well in school, engaged in relatively benign acts of mischief or rebellion, participated in scouting and sports, and spent long, leisurely summers at the ocean. Her three sons and two daughters are all high achievers: two lawyers, a successful business owner, an accountant, and a teacher. Surprisingly in this day and age, all five are married. Sophie has eleven grandchildren.

Sophie, for some ineffable reason, makes you feel better just by being in her presence. At eighty-five she is spry and fit and looks like the quintessential grandmother from a Norman Rockwell painting. She has lively blue eyes, pure white hair, and one of the most extraordinarily positive attitudes I have ever encountered.

This robust, outgoing persona is reflected in the way she describes her relationships with her children. "I can't explain it, exactly, why my family life was as happy as it was," she says. "I always enjoyed being a mother, even during the difficult parts. Everything—being home for them after school, listening to their problems, living through their new boyfriends and girlfriends and the breakups, all that. And now, watching the family extend down to grandchildren. I have promised all my grandchildren a trip to Europe when they get to high school, and I've done that with four of them so far." Sophie describes her life today as a busy round of family events and visits, attending most of the anniversaries, birthdays, weddings, and graduations.

But when we get to the issue of differences among her children, she only hesitates a moment: "You're not going to tell the kids, right?" When I assure her that I won't, she immediately delivers judgment: "Alice. She's the one. I have always gotten along the best with her. We share the same interests, we talk easily, and we confide in one another. Oh, I love all of them and they're all great. But Alice is a little different. She's the one I'm most comfortable with. If I ever had to live with one of them, it would be Alice." I hazard a question: Does she think her children know she feels this way? "Oh, of course not! Your kids are going to be different, and you'll feel differently about each one. What you do—this is one of *my* life lessons—is *never show it.*"

And that's precisely what successful parents manage to do throughout the course of family life. They accept as a fact of life that they like some of their children more than the others. They envision an abstract level of "love," on which all their children are equals. I learned from the experts that the blanket statement "I love all of my children equally" is entirely consistent with the truth "but I like one of them more than the others." The experts who manage this ambivalence accept their preferences, don't obsess about it, and by all means *do not show it.*

When Jill Suitor and I looked at our data from the study of mothers and children and analyzed it using sophisticated social science methods, I learned precisely how true this is. The majority of the older parents are in fact highly successful at both having favorites and keeping their children in the dark. As we saw earlier, most moms picked a child to whom they were the most emotionally close—essentially the one she liked best. And in a sizeable majority of families, these children didn't know the mother's preference.

In many cases the children responded that their mother had no favorite (even though she did). When children believed that their mother did have a favorite, we asked them who that special child was. And in many instances—surprise, surprise—the child identified himself or herself as the favorite offspring. And more often than not, *they were wrong.* So we have a pattern in which parents have favorites, but they skillfully keep how they feel from their offspring.

And this is a very good thing. There are decades of research on parental favoritism, with many studies looking at the effects on both young children and adolescents. The news about obvious favoritism is bad: when children perceive that treatment of siblings in the family is unequal, they are more likely to have conduct problems, poorer mental health, and to engage in delinquent behaviors earlier. In addition, children who view their parents as playing favorites have more conflict with their siblings and have less happy and supportive relationships with them. Our research shows that these problems persist among adult children of older parents.

In my interviews with America's elders, no other topic revealed more raw emotion and reservoirs of remembered hurt than the experience of parental favoritism. Some experts—separated from their childhoods by sixty, seventy, or even eighty years—choked up as they recalled the effects of obvious and damaging preference for a sibling. There's no better argument for working hard to treat your children as equally and as fairly as possible.

Loraine Bauer, eighty-nine, was born in the rural South on a poor and isolated farm. She joked, "It was so far back in the swamp that we had to swing in on grapevines. They counted the rings on my legs to find out how old I was. So what I'm saying is—there was not a lot of contact outside of the farm." Her memories of childhood are colored by recollections of parental favoritism that influenced the course of her life.

> I HAD YOUNGER BROTHERS who were my parents' favorites. And I think that framed my life to a great deal. I don't mean they didn't love me—it's just sons were important and girls were only to marry and produce more sons. And I grew up with the feeling that "I'll show you I'm better than you, boy." And be damned to you. I made some achievements in life, education, that kind of thing. But when I had gotten there, I wondered why I bothered. Kind of sad, isn't it?

Her grandparents helped her deal with her second-class treatment in the family:

> I HAD MY GRANDMOTHER, who was really the guiding influence in my life because I knew she loved me and without reservation. My grandfather too was very loving and taught me to accept the way I look. He used to pick me up in his horse and buggy and take me out for rides. And we'd sit and look out and eat strawberries. And he pulled me by my pigtails and he said, "That's all right, honey. You're like my mother." And he said, "You're going to be a pistol."
>
> For my parents, the boys were important. And I was the oldest and scrawny and redheaded. They were blond and blue-eyed. Parents need to be loving and accepting of all their children—I was a different child and I don't think they understood that—to be accepting of whatever the child is, and that's sometimes very hard.

Parental preference for a sibling may not seem like a big deal, even when it results in sibling rivalry. But it has another potentially devastating effect: it leads siblings to become distant from one another. Rather than sharing time, experiences, and memories with a brother or sister in later life, early favoritism can cause estrangement. At seventy-eight, memories of her mother's disparate treatment of her children still distress Marianne Ratliff.

> WHAT HAVE I LEARNED about child rearing? My goodness, that's a tough one. I learned that mothers don't always like their children. Not voluntarily, it just somehow happens that way, and I happened to be the one amongst them that Mother did not like. I learned that I never wanted my chil-

dren to grow up in the same kind of situation—that was probably the most important lesson. I learned that you shouldn't always believe that person who doesn't like you and what she says about you. Her favoritism also affected my relationships with my siblings. I have learned that my siblings can be cruel. I have learned from that to exclude them from my life.

Parental favoritism and unfair treatment affected some experts in other ways, making social and work relationships difficult later in life. Ron Gomez, seventy-eight, has spent a lifetime dealing with the aftereffects of parental favoritism.

I WAS THE FIRST baby born into an extended family, and we shared a house with my grandparents and my aunts lived nearby. And of course I was the apple of everybody's eyes already, and when my brother came along they didn't pay any attention to him. Late in his life, my father told me, "When Peter came along and nobody paid attention to him, I had to favor him."

As a child I knew there was something wrong, and I didn't know what because I fought with my brother and I had terrible problems with my father. Then I understood what the favoritism did. You can't play favorites as a parent, and I understood that in some sort of a vague way as a two- or three-year-old. I acted up, and my father got angry with me because I was so difficult. This made for a terrible childhood. My brother and I fought terribly— once I lost a front tooth. My mother was almost invisible in all this. I spent three years with a psychiatrist to get over this, when I realized that my family history was affecting my work life.

It's certainly helpful when the experts give us such clear guidance on an issue. Here they offer two important and intertwined life lessons that parents of all ages should take very seriously.

Part one of this lesson is that some degree of parental favoritism is normal. You almost certainly can't avoid it, and it's probably fruitless to try. Children are people, with distinct personalities. We like people who are similar to us, and chances are you are going to feel closer to the kid who is the most like you in personality, leisure-time preferences, and values. All the reasons why we find one person very appealing and another less so apply as much within families as they do outside them. The lesson from the experts is to give up worrying about it—feeling closer to one child than to another is normal, natural, and nothing to feel guilty about.

The second part of the lesson says to take all those honest feelings about your kids that you have come to accept—*and bury them deep*. You can have your preferences. You can perhaps talk to your spouse about them with the bedroom door closed. But keep them from your kids. Avoid making any comparisons that favor one child over the other. There are ninety-year-olds who never forgot their parents saying things like "He's my pride, but he's my joy" or "She's the pretty one, and she's the smart one." As a parent you may *think* this kind of thing, but among the most harmful family experiences the elders described was feeling that they were the unfavored child. The experts tell us that honesty isn't the best policy when it comes to preference for one child over another.

The Third Lesson: Don't Hit Your Kids

I can hear some of you asking, "Isn't this lesson outdated?" Haven't parents moved beyond the days when children were spanked aplenty and no one thought twice about it? No, indeed they haven't. Despite changing attitudes toward parenting, physical punishment of children remains the norm in most families—indeed it is "deviant" never to hit one's children. Studies show that over 90 percent of parents of three- to five-year-olds report using corporal punishment in the preceding year, and although the numbers decline after age five, nearly half of parents still report having slapped or hit their twelve-year-olds in the past year. These statistics vary among different groups in the population, but most parents still strike their children and for some it is a first choice of discipline rather than a last resort.

The view from later life is that physical punishment of children is nothing any of us will be proud of as we look back on our parenting. The experts' lesson? It should be avoided or, at worst, be an unusual (and regretted) event. This lesson was one of the great surprises for me in writing this book. I had stereotyped the experts as belonging to the "spare the rod and spoil the child" generation, but only a minority expressed such views. Instead I found most of the experts to be wary of physical punishment for a variety of reasons.

One group of experts rarely or never used physical punishment, and not one regretted that decision. Peter Mortimer, eighty-eight, told me, "Well, I think we expected and received respect from our children. I never laid a hand on them because we were respectful in our household from the start."

Bonnie Gilbreath, sixty-seven, was emphatic: "You have to do two things: first you've got to love the child so that you want the child to succeed, and then you've got to listen to what the child is saying about what he wants to do. I might have lost my temper once or twice and given one or the other a shake, but that's one thing my husband and I tried never to do if we could help it. That's not love, no matter what people say."

Edith O'Connor, seventy-six, raised seven children with her husband Ed. She told me that they were united on one thing: avoiding harsh discipline.

> I THINK YOU HAVE to agree on the kind of discipline that you will enforce with your children and be together on that as a husband and wife. You have to control your anger. I think that the more that you can talk with them and explain life to them, the better. One thing that bothers me the most is when a family is out someplace and you hear the parents yelling at their children. I think that discipline should be very quiet and controlled, but kind. I know that my mother would never discipline us. She'd just look at us, and we'd know that we should do the right thing. That's what I mean. You don't have to yell about it.

Many of the other experts had used physical punishment but reported that it wasn't particularly effective and that they wouldn't recommend it. They viewed hitting as a failure in parenting rather than a technique to be recommended to younger parents.

Janice Lea, eighty-six, was married in 1945 and had a son and a daughter. Life was difficult when her children were young: "My first husband became an alcoholic, we were divorced, and I was left with two children and so I made it on my own." She so deeply regrets using physical punishment that she asked for her adult children's forgiveness:

> WELL, I SPANKED MY kids but I would not do that now. I would advise against spanking. I think time-outs and denying them certain things is a better way to go than to hit them. I don't believe in that anymore, but I did spank my kids. My son, he was a very quiet person and he didn't really

show a lot of emotion, and we just get along great. I don't know whether he was always happy with me, but he never raised his voice with me even though I had spanked him when he was little. But I apologized to them and told them that I was sorry that I did it.

Don't get me wrong: the experts believe in firmness, in maintaining a clear moral compass, and in setting limits. But they are remarkably unified on the idea that corporal punishment of children is a disciplinary dead end that spoils the relationship, leaving emotional marks that last long after childhood.

Rosemary Brewster is a very sensible ninety-year-old. She raised three daughters and a son. The experience wasn't always easy: "The kids never gave me any problems, except the boy." Despite her son's willfulness, she quickly gave up on physical punishment. Here's our conversation about it, which couldn't be more succinct:

I asked, "Did you believe in spanking your kids?"

"Not really," she replied, "It doesn't do much good."

"How so?"

"It only hurts you. You feel really bad about doing it. It's not doing any good, so why do it?"

This is the experts' advice in a nutshell: if it makes you feel bad, and it doesn't do any good, why do it?

It turns out that the accumulated wisdom of America's elders is firmly in line with current scientific research. Prominent child-development researchers are nearly unanimous on the negative effects of corporal punishment of children over the course of life. Among young children, those who are physically punished show more aggression and antisocial behavior. And the more often and the more severely a child is slapped or hit, the greater the negative effects on mental health and likelihood of behavior problems. Studies show that corporal punishment is related to poorer relationships with parents in adolescence and into adulthood. Most disturbing, children who have received frequent physical punishment are more likely to engage in abusive behavior toward their own spouses and/or children in adulthood.

So let's listen to the experts on this one. Their basic message about physical punishment is, Why do it? When you look back from your seventies or eighties, hitting your kids is something you won't remember with pride, and you will almost certainly wish you hadn't done it. Plenty of the elders (one-third or more) did just fine without falling back in frustration on spanking, slapping, or hitting. And their kids turned out fine. So the next time the urge arises to settle a discipline problem with a good, hard smack, the experts would counsel you to think twice, or three times, or long enough that you don't do it.

The Fourth Lesson: Avoid a Rift at All Costs

Stop for a moment and think about your kids, about how much time, effort, and expense you are investing in them. Let's say it's a son. Consider how you might be spending your time if you weren't using it to change his diapers, or to work an extra job to pay for his piano lessons, or to devote weekends to cheer him on at the soccer field. More important, take a minute to get in touch with the immense attachment you feel to him, the way you light up when you come home to him in the evening, and the rush of joy from hearing "Mommy's home!" or "Daddy's home!" when you are reunited after an absence. Consider the day-to-day activities you engage in with him, the pleasure you feel in his achievements, the comfort you both receive from quietly holding him at the end of the day.

Now project yourself forward thirty-five years. Your son is well into adulthood and you are the age of the experts. Imagine that this child, in whom you have invested so much love and hope, *is no longer part of your life*. Not that he is dead, but rather that you no longer have any relationship with him. He may live nearby, perhaps even in the same city, but you are in fact "dead" to one another. For a small but significant number of the experts, this is reality. They are alienated from a child, so deeply estranged from him or her that the separation seems irrevocable.

Among the saddest people I met were those living with such a situation. No matter how long it had gone on or what the specific circumstances were, the destruction of the parent-child bond was a persistent source of melancholy, a feeling of incompleteness that weighed down the soul. And one failed relationship is not necessarily mitigated by having warm, fulfilling ties with other offspring. Almost all the experts with a child who was "lost" to them or with whom there was "bad blood" felt unresolved or incomplete. And such feelings only became more acute as they neared the end of life.

For this book and other studies I've conducted, I've sifted through thousands of detailed interviews about child rearing. Among mothers, fathers, and children alike, one clear and compelling insight emerges from the many accounts of permanent separation from a child: do everything you can to avoid *the rift*.

The word "rift," when applied to the social world, is defined as a rupture in relationships resulting in personal separation. Its geological definition, however, evokes even more effectively the effects described by the experts: "a crack or splitting into two or more fragments, as a result of force, a blow, or strain." Visualize a fissure in rock; the split is dramatic and virtually irreparable. This is indeed how some experts described their relationship with an estranged child.

The rift and its repercussions are sources of some of the most painful what-ifs and if-onlys that the experts reported. There are a variety of causes of rifts. In some families they result from a parent's or child's lifestyle choice. A parent's divorce in later life, for example, might prompt a child to cease contact out of anger. Children not fulfilling parents' expectations during a health crisis is a cause of resentment among some, as is a child "marrying the wrong person." A child's coming out as gay or lesbian is felt to be intolerable by some older parents. And an act of dishonesty or perceived betrayal of trust can be a source of rifts. The common thread in all these cases is the decision on the part of parent, child, or both that something irrevocable has occurred involving betrayal, humiliation, anger, or indifference.

Susan Lemieux, a petite and lively eighty-five-year-old, greeted me from her wheelchair and eagerly invited me to sit down. We talked about her life as one of twelve children growing up in the rural South, her work, and her two marriages. Widowed in her fifties after a happy first marriage, Susan remarried in her early sixties. The second relationship was very fulfilling for her, filled with extensive travel throughout the world—an opportunity she had missed in her previous relationship because of job and financial restrictions.

Susan, despite a daunting array of health problems, was a funny, enthusiastic interviewee. She likes a drink (bourbon and Coke) every now and then and enjoys activities with friends in her assisted living community. Reflecting back over her experiences, she told me, "I think I've had a good life. I think I came through it real good."

But when I asked, "What advice would you have for people about relationships with their grown children?" the atmosphere changed in an instant. Susan became very still, holding her breath. Then words exploded from her, and she pounded her hands in frustration on the arms of her chair.

> I DON'T KNOW, I don't know! I did something wrong—I'll tell you right now! Because I don't hear from either one of my kids. I don't even—I never hear from them. And it hurts like crazy. Why do you think that is? Do you have any idea?

She continued, choking back tears and shaking her head from side to side:

> I DON'T KNOW WHY. I don't know. With Grace, her life is so outlandish. I never know where she is because she travels all the time and she's done that for years. She married and didn't stay married long, and has been single twenty years. I understand she has a live-in boyfriend now, but I don't know anything about him. I just know that there is such a thing.

Although Susan initially stated that she didn't know why the rift occurred, it turned out that she could pinpoint a probable cause:

> I THINK WHEN I married the second time it was such a different life from how we had lived before. And I was so busy, and we were going all the time, so I lost track of them. I stopped being close to them. They weren't exactly unhappy about it—we just had nothing in common anymore. And I think that's where it started, because after my first husband died it just never was the same. Their children were

about high school age or getting up into the ages where they're beginning to rebel, and I think probably their time with their children moved them away from me and we just never connected again.

They were close to their father. They idolized him, in fact. And after I married again, they just didn't have anything in common with my second husband. It was such a different way of life. And I think that's where it began. But I do wish I'd hear from them more often now, yes I do!

With her health problems, Susan sees the end of life on the horizon. She tried to reach out:

ABOUT A MONTH AGO, I wrote both of those kids a long letter and I never heard back from them. And I call them from time to time. I never catch up with Grace. All I ever get is the answering machine. With the other one, I've talked to him—oh, every couple of months I'll call and talk for a few minutes, but we have so little in common that we just talk about the grandkids.

By the time I ended the interview, Susan had recovered and was back to telling me colorful anecdotes about her long life. But I've never forgotten the anguish in her voice as she told me, "I did something wrong . . . And it hurts like crazy."

I learned from the experts that the rift can happen to anyone and in any family. So I was keenly interested in what they believe people can do about it. In my large sample of elders I had access both to individuals who had suffered the rift and to those who had lived through a near miss—a situation in which a relationship rupture almost occurred but the family came back from the brink. The experts offered three tips for "rift prevention," not all of them necessarily easy but that need to be taken seriously.

Tip 1: See the potential rift early and defuse it.

The experts acknowledge that once the rift sets in, it takes on a life of its own and becomes much more difficult to repair. Indeed they had less useful counsel regarding how to rebuild a relationship after the fact. The time to act, they suggest, is when the early warning signs show themselves.

Martha Fulkerson, seventy-one, nearly lost contact with her son Jay after he married Riva—by all accounts a very difficult person. Martha and Jay had been very close throughout their lives, sharing many interests and activities. This led to jealousy and outbursts of anger on Riva's part. Finally a major blowup occurred about a relatively trivial issue—whether Martha would accompany them on a short vacation. Jay had invited her but Riva strongly and publicly objected. Martha retreated, hurt and angry. This event led to increasing estrangement and being nearly cut off from the couple.

Martha reported: "I should never have let things deteriorate the way they did. Looking back on it, I could see problems brewing and I probably helped make Riva jealous. I couldn't hold back from criticizing her to Jay sometimes. I now see our big fight as a ticking time bomb. Nothing was worth getting to this point." Parents of high schoolers to middle-aged sons and daughters need to ask themselves seriously, "Is this battle worth it?" The experts say that usually it's not.

Tip 2: Act immediately after the rift occurs.

The experts told me that the viewpoints of both parties harden quickly and in a relatively short time it becomes easier *not* to make the effort to reconcile than to try to do so. The new reality sets in fast; therefore the time to "make things better" is as soon as possible after the blowup.

Janice Carpenter, seventy-seven, had always had a somewhat tense relationship with her elder daughter Gloria, although she enjoyed warm companionship with her younger daughter, Beth. Things came to a head when Gloria decided to go on vacation instead of attending the wedding of Beth's only daughter. The anger she felt ruined the event for Janice, and the money she had sacrificed for the wedding felt wasted. When Gloria returned from her vacation, Janice refused to speak to her, becoming angrier with each passing day. According to Janice, this event was the "last straw," a turning point at which she "saw Gloria's true colors." She felt humiliated in front of her closest friends and relatives and began to speak of Gloria's behavior as "unforgivable." For her part, Gloria felt fully justified in her behavior and had difficulty understanding "what the fuss is all about."

Looking back at the rift, Janice reported, "I should have had a heart-to-heart with Gloria right away. After a week or two, we were both so angry, and I guess hardened, that it was terribly difficult even to start a conversation." Days turned into weeks, and over time Gloria simply got used to the lack of contact. Recently Beth has worked successfully to reinstate contact between her mother and sister, but all agree that the situation would have been greatly eased had a frank and honest discussion taken place immediately after the rift occurred.

That's what happened in the Gallegos family. Although he lived nearby, James Gallegos failed to help his mother, eighty-two-year-old Maria, when her husband suffered a stroke. When he died several weeks later, Maria found her anger toward her son to be so intense that she was alarmed. She decided she would act as soon as possible, sensing that the situation would only get worse. Within a week, she sat down with James and told him exactly how she felt. James confessed that he was so upset by his father's illness that he was incapable of helping out. Maria, although still harboring some resentment at what she felt was James's selfishness, allowed the reconciliation to take place. "It's worth it," she said, "not to feel like I might lose what I have that's good with my son."

Tip 3: When all else fails, it's the parent who usually needs to compromise.

I am well aware that this recommendation sounds unfair; however, in my review of accounts of intergenerational rifts I've found that it's usually the parent who pays the higher price if a rift occurs. Mothers and fathers simply have a greater level of investment in their children than the reverse. Indeed gerontologists call this the "intergenerational stake"— parents tend to need and to value the relationship with the child more and therefore stand to lose more by letting the relationship deteriorate or disintegrate. Particularly acute is the potential distance or separation from grandchildren that can occur as a result of the rift.

One of the more difficult experiences in relationships with adult children involves an area that was unchartered territory for most of the experts: a son or daughter coming out as gay or lesbian. Surveys show that tolerance of same-sex preference is strongly related to age. For example, 60 percent of Americans age eighteen to twenty-nine support marriage for gays and lesbians, compared to 25 percent of people age sixty-five and older. Similarly, 55 percent of the younger group supports adoption rights by gays and lesbians, compared to 25 percent of the older group. Although there is no survey data that I am aware of, acceptance of gays and lesbians during the experts' formative years (1920–1950) was minuscule. Such issues simply weren't discussed.

Therefore, grappling with a son or daughter being gay or lesbian, meeting and interacting with a same-sex partner, and somehow integrating this foreign concept into a very different worldview required a major adjustment for most experts in this situation. In some cases, unfortunately, it led to a rift in which the parents could not find a way to deal with their disappointment that the child's life had taken such an unexpected turn.

However, some parents—even conservative ones—came to terms with precisely this situation and avoided the rift. There weren't many more traditional men among the experts than Mike Hoyt, seventy-six, whose life had revolved around work, family, and sports. But he and his wife managed to change their views dramatically when their son informed them about his sexuality.

OUR SON WAS GAY, and when he first told us, our reaction—and my reaction in particular—was very negative. It was very upsetting because I just couldn't figure it out. "Oh boy," I said, "that's going to hurt us in the community," which was a terrible, selfish thing to say. It was stupid. But, you know, when you're ignorant of a situation, those are the things that happen, I guess. I still regret that comment.

It took me a long time to accept meeting his partner. I had a tough time with that. But when I met him, he turned out to be a very successful businessman in town and a super-nice guy, and the further it went along, the more I accepted him and felt more comfortable being around him, until it came to the point where it was not even a factor.

And I think one of the experiences that came out of that was we became much more tolerant and understanding of the gay community and his partner and so forth. They're wonderful people. Most of them are very, very successful.

My other children were very good, very accepting of my son's situation, from day one, which is very helpful. And the grandchildren, you wouldn't even know there was anything different about this relationship. For them it was just not a problem.

The love they had for their son ultimately overcame the potential rift. "Our son was a very, very wonderful guy, very caring. He was very well thought of. He had a great compassion for people, particularly the less fortunate. He just had a certain compassion about him."

Tragically, the Hoyts' son died suddenly. The grieving process was made easier by the knowledge that they had enjoyed a decade of warm relationships with their son and his partner. And the relationship didn't end: "In fact, we still have dinner. We go out and we socialize with his partner a lot. We're very close with him. He's like family."

It's one thing to say "avoid the rift." But what happens when something seems unforgivable? Can a parent (and the relationship) recover? Some experts have had the worst happen, stood on the brink of the rift, and decided that it still wasn't worth the end of the relationship with the child.

When asked about her adult children, Gwen Hagerman, seventy-three, replied, "My daughter and I are close." But a long pause followed; I could sense that there was a story there and that Gwen was deciding whether or not to tell it. Finally it came out:

MY DAUGHTER HAD AN affair with my second husband. And I was absolutely devastated, and he tried to convince me I was crazy, but I knew that I wasn't, and she admitted the truth. And for a few years we were estranged. But then, what do you do? I could have turned against her, but I thought, "My God, this is the only daughter I have!" And I realized that she wasn't entirely to blame. This second husband was a pretty bad guy.

And so, you let bygones be bygones. You can't dwell on the past and you can't be bitter, because in the long run the only person you hurt is yourself. We got back together primarily because I was helping her take care of her children, whom I adored, and we're friends today. We get along quite well. You have to let things go. They're over and done with—you can't do anything about it, so let it be.

This is an important message for parents of any age: *avoid the rift*. The issue that threatens to divide you and one of your children can occur early or late in life. Of course it is possible that a child's behavior is so damaging or abusive that a separation is needed for a parent's physical or mental health. But the experts tell us that rifts most often occur over matters that seem important at the time but are almost never worth the ultimate pain of separation.

The Fifth Lesson:
Take a Lifelong View of Relationships with Children

Through my conversations with hundreds of older people, I discovered a new phase of life that I call the "middle-aged blur." The years of raising young children and adolescents, roughly from age thirty to fifty, are frequently described as precisely that: a blur, a rush of activity so hectic that when it's done the entire experience seems to have passed in an instant. From the birth of the first child, the intersection of work, family life, and school becomes a black hole that devours time, energy, and reflection. Most parents are so "in the moment" during those years that it is difficult for them to step back and be reflective amid the whirlwind of activity.

And here's where the special wisdom of the experts comes to the fore, because it emerges from *having lived their lives*. For those of you in the midst of child rearing, try imagining that you are the age of the experts. If child rearing can be compared to a marathon, you've reached the finish line.

You've experienced the highs and the lows of raising a child, from the transcendent awe of birth through sleepless nights with a baby and into the daily excitement (and aggravation) of toddler-hood. You've worried about childhood illnesses, about grades, about that questionable magazine you found under your son's bed (and wisely never mentioned), about your daughter's first solo drive behind the wheel of a car. You've experienced exhilaration: the game-winning basket in the last minute of overtime, the unex-pected late-night conversation when you and your teenager for once really connected, the fat envelope from a good college that arrived in April (after a few thin ones arrived first). And you have said good-bye and watched your children leave home, as we all must.

But what happens then? Because at the moment your son or daughter leaves the house, the unexpected question pops up: what do we do with the rest of our lives? All our energy has been invested in the successful launch of the child into the "real world" such that there's been little time to look at the bigger picture. Most people in the United States become parents in their mid or late twenties. The blessed event is followed by eighteen years in which they share a roof with that child. By the time he or she sallies forth into an in-dependent life, Mom and Dad are in their midforties. And they are likely to live for another forty years or more.

You do the math. Most of the time we spend as parents is not when kids are dependents in the family home but when they are adults. The huge growth in the average life span has created a demographic trend the world has never seen before: the long, shared lifetimes of parents and their adult offspring. In the old days, parents were much more likely to die fairly soon after their last child reached adulthood (or even before). Now we can reap the rewards (and the challenges) of the relationships we've created for decades.

If I add up my interviews with the experts and all the other studies I've been involved in with older parents, it probably amounts to around ten thousand interviews over the years. And I've learned that most parents are focused in the immediate moment when they are raising children at home. They are in the trenches, and those eighteen years go by in the middle-aged blur. What my studies suggest, however, is that parents need to keep in mind what comes after. What are you doing when your child is age five, ten, or fifteen that will create a lasting, loving relationship over the much longer time of his or her adulthood and your middle and old age?

Because, believe me, as your life goes on *you will want your children there*. I wrote earlier about the enormous pain troubled and estranged relationships cause older people. When you are in your seventies and beyond, your children provide you with continuity, meaning, attachment, and ultimately an overarching sense of a greater purpose in life. If they are not there spending time with you, keeping up with your activities and you with theirs, and ultimately serving as a source of support, old age can be a very tough time indeed. You've made the investment. From midlife on, you will deeply desire what I call "the payoff."

You've heard about the rift and its consequences. But invest wisely and well in your relationships with your children—spending time with them even if it means sacrifice, avoiding harsh discipline, mending disagreements before they become rifts—and there is indeed a payoff beyond price. Rather than preach at you, I'll allow the experts to do the talking. When you've done all you can to nurture and maintain the best relationships possible with your children, you can reap rewards. Like anything else, the investment brings payoffs like these.

Ray Caddell, eighty, is a widower with two sons and two daughters. He and his late wife, Marjorie, invested time and love in them throughout their childhood, building strong relationships and pleasant memories, even if it meant sacrificing career opportunities. The payoff? Ray says:

MY RELATIONSHIPS WITH THE four children are a source of pure joy. I love to have them around. They all like each other very much, and they like each others' spouses and families. It's a source of just pure joy.

One of the things they did recently was on my eightieth birthday, last June. Before that I'd had a conversation with one of the kids. I just happened to mention that before I depart this vale of tears I'd like to go to Florida for baseball spring training. So they gave me that trip, with just the four of them. The two girls approached it with a little bit of fear and trembling: "Do I really want this much baseball?" But they did it for me. And they have subsequently said that they enjoyed it so much. That's just the camaraderie we have as a family.

Essie Feist is ninety-nine years old. She is astonishingly active: she swims and walks for exercise (and only recently stopped driving), knits, and maintains an active social life. "And I have two wonderful daughters. They're a blessing for me now. They live nearby. So it's nice." Her daughters' ages: seventy-six and sixty-nine.

The payoff:

WHEN THEY WERE LITTLE, my belief was "keep your home open." Let them bring in friends so you know who they associate with. You want to be sure that they're taken care of. You can't let them just run. They were good children. I saw to it that they got to school, that they did their homework. You have to work at it. It's very important for parents to take care of their children. And like I say, keep an open mind. Leave your door open for their friends so you know who they're playing with and you know where they are and what they are doing.

Getting along with them as adults? It's easy—we love each other and take care of each other. And I think you learn from your children too as you go along. I've learned a lot from my children. The world has changed. You can close your mind. So instead you listen, you look, and you try to listen to them, hear what they're saying.

One of Essie's daughters spoke up:

AND WE STILL HAVE fun with her! Every other Sunday my husband and I play pinochle with her. We play cutthroat pinochle. And very often she wins. We don't let her win, because we were brought up to believe that when you win it's because you really win. So we still play that way. So when she wins, she really wins. And she's sharp. You can't put one over on her. She keeps us in line. At our age she still keeps us in line.

As you make decisions regarding child rearing, think about the payoff in the long run. An old expression tells us, "We must do now that which will profit us in the future." The experts' lessons reflect that sentiment. Consider actions toward your children (both when they are young and when they are adults) in the long term. When you are in your later years, you are likely to have one simple desire regarding your children: that they like you and wish to be around you. According to the experts, actions that get in the way of that future should be vigorously avoided. Essie has had parent-child relationships for more than seven decades. You may too, so make decisions now that will lead to the payoff that Essie, Ray, and many other experts have received.

Postscript:
Abandon Perfection

In the first chapter of this book, I laid out the argument for listening to the life lessons that the oldest Americans have to offer. This chapter on child rearing highlights precisely why taking heed of the experts' unique perspective can be so valuable. There are some things that only become clear later in life, after there has been time to see them play out. That's where these five lessons from the experts come in.

Here's the refrigerator list:

1. **It's all about time.** Sacrifice if necessary to spend the maximum amount of time possible with your children. You and your children need to be together in the flow of daily household life and not just during planned "quality time."

2. **It's normal to have favorites, but never show it.** Accept that you may have favorites among your children, but do not ever let them know.

3. **Don't hit your kids.** Discipline your children in a loving, respectful way that excludes physical punishment (no matter how tempting it may be in the short term).

4. **Avoid a rift at all costs.** Do everything necessary to avoid a permanent rift with a child—even if it requires compromise on a parent's part.

5. **Take a lifelong view of relationships with children.** Parenthood goes on long after kids leave home, so make decisions when they are young that will lead to positive relationships in the second half of life.

As I reflected on these lessons, I became aware of an underlying message these experienced parents wished to convey to us. From their vantage point, they were asking us to resist one of the cardinal temptations of American parents: the search for perfection, both in our children and in our own parenting.

Logically, most of us recognize the futility of creating perfect children. Indeed these days the "quest for the perfect child" conjures the specter of using genetic techniques to craft flawless offspring. However, centuries of parenting experience show the futility of that idea: as soon as we subject this hypothetical engineered child to the vagaries of family life, to our inevitable imperfections and mistakes, and to the barely controllable environments created by siblings, all bets are off.

And yet most parents hold themselves up to some kind of perfect standard when they evaluate their parenting. "If only," they say, "I had encouraged Johnny more with music, he would have used his talents." "If only I had provided more opportunities for Mary to play with other children, she wouldn't be so shy." Of course many of the if-onlys work two ways: "If only I had pushed Jimmy harder with his studies, he would have done better in school" can ring just as true as "If only I *hadn't* pushed Jimmy so hard, he would have done better in school."

In addition we hold up children to impossible standards,

comparing them to ideals of well-behaved, hardworking young-sters that exist in our imaginations alone. It has become a cliché—the child who is shuttled from dance class to language class to volunteer job and needs a (parental) scheduler as badly as a corporate CEO. Most of us have also seen the less-than-gifted B student whose parents insist on testing to show a "learn-ing disability," the expensive individual coaching for the kid who doesn't make the soccer team, and the costly summer enrich-ment courses that fill the dormitories and coffers of universities each summer.

The experts' response to this pressure allows us to breathe a sigh of relief. Because they will be the first to tell you: *no one has perfect children*. They admit it: all of their kids had at least some difficulty, a flaw, a period of unhappiness, a major wrong turn. The reassuring thing is that most of their kids turned out pretty well nevertheless. The message is clear: abandon all thoughts of raising the "perfect child" or being the perfect parent, and do it as early as possible. They echo the pioneering child psychologist Donald Win-nicott, who assured mothers and fathers that what they should as-pire to is "good-enough parenting." We can't be perfect, but we can be "good enough" to raise decent, loving children.

Gertrude Towers, seventy-six, told me:

WELL, IT'S FUNNY BECAUSE we brought up our children in the time of Dr. Spock. That was a household book that you went to, to find out what we were doing wrong or doing right. We were going to have perfect children, and we were going to be perfect parents. It doesn't work that way.

Being a good-enough parent means allowing kids to fail. When asked about raising children, Lenore Fruchter's first words are, "It's a hard job." This doesn't mean that Lenore, seventy-eight, didn't enjoy raising her three children. It simply acknowledges that many challenges arise in the course of parenting. She has thought a great deal about children and child rearing, having worked as a teacher and then become a well-known children's book author. Her message: abandon the quest for the perfect child and let them learn from what they do wrong.

MY HUSBAND AND I have the same attitude about our kids: we put them in situations where they could make decisions, and they didn't always make the right ones but they learned from their mistakes and that's important. If you never make a mistake, you never know there's a right or a wrong way to do things. It may not always be for the best, but you learn how to deal with difficulties.

I remember once saying to my son, "I wonder what you kids would've done if we had been different as parents, like parents who pushed their kids into a particular college and ran their lives." He looked at me in total surprise and said, "Look, we've all gone to college, we all have good jobs, we have jobs that are not hurting anyone, and we're not in jail and we're done with the drug scene—what else would you have wanted from us?" And I said, "You're right, I don't want anything else from you." Pushing for perfection doesn't work, in my experience.

The experts tell you that you can lighten up regarding your children: relax your expectations and assume that failure is inevitable at times. Dealing with problems in a supportive way is what counts, not an ideal of perfection. Allow the accumulated expert wisdom to give you permission to give up perfection in exchange for being "good enough." None of the experts' five lessons requires perfection, just openness, the ability to listen, and good intentions. And those are qualities all parents can develop.

CHAPTER 5

❖ ❖ ❖

Find the Magic

Lessons for Aging Fearlessly and Well

Edwina Elbert, 94

MY ADVICE TO PEOPLE about growing old? I'd tell them to find the magic. The world is a magical place in lots of ways. To enjoy getting up in the morning and watching the sun come up. And that's something that you can do when you are growing older. You can be grateful, happy for the things that have happened. You should enjoy your life. Grow a little. Just because you're getting older doesn't mean that you need to stop growing. I used to think that when you got old you sat back in a rocking chair and let the world go by. Well, that's not for me and that's not for a lot of people. I can't dance anymore, but if I could I would.

There's no reason for anybody in this world to ever be bored. That's one thing I've always said. Well, if I died and went to heaven, I'd be bored to death with how they say heaven is. There's no need for you to be bored in this world. There's so much out there.

DURING THE GEORGE W. Bush era, I was interviewed by the *Washington Post* for an article about the president's sixtieth birthday. George W. had spent the previous weeks, in the words of the reporter, "griping about getting old." The article explained:

IN RECENT MONTHS, BUSH, in speech after speech, has referred to himself as the "old president, getting older by the minute," as one of "the gray-haired folks," as "getting older" and as just flat-out "old."

Asked to opine as a gerontologist, I commented:

FOR MANY BOOMERS, TURNING 60 is a fairly significant shock . . . The generation that believed it would be young forever, clearly will not. The boomers are having a hard time with the existential reality of life not being one open-ended opportunity after another.

When the article came out, I had an "aha!" moment. Although I had been talking about the baby boomers in a general way, I suddenly realized that I had actually been describing *myself* and my own deep-seated fears about aging. I am the quintessential boomer, born in 1954, precisely in the middle of that huge wave of births that began when GIs returned from World War II and started large families. From cowboy outfits to hula hoops to crowded elementary school classrooms to fears about "the bomb" to TV culture to the strange inability to remember parts of the late 1960s—I experienced it all.

If there is one stereotypical—and generally true—image of the baby boom generation, it is a deeply entrenched Peter Pan attitude: boomers have great difficulty comprehending the reality of growing old. They are of course matched in this by the Generation Xers and Yers who followed them, who also firmly deny the aging process. But boomers started the "youth is forever" craze, epitomized by the Yippie Jerry Rubin's slogan "Don't trust anyone over thirty" (as if he would never get there) and Pete Townshend's line in the Who's classic anthem "My Generation": "I hope I die before I get old!" (Now that Pete's turned sixty-five, one wonders if he still feels the same way).

So how does a youth-oriented culture like ours come to terms with aging? Lurking behind the wine tours, the adventure travel, the red sports car, and the second or third marriage is the knowledge of the inevitability of old age. No one has surpassed the couplet penned by the seventeenth-century statesman and poet Andrew Marvell:

> But at my back I always hear
> Time's winged chariot hurrying near.

Or as the existentialist philosopher Albert Camus put it:

A DAY COMES WHEN a man notices that . . . [h]e belongs to time, and by the horror that seizes him, he recognizes his worst enemy.

Fear of aging is rampant in our society. Surveys over the past two decades show the pervasive negative attitudes Americans hold about aging. Psychologist Todd D. Nelson, an expert on the topic, sums up the research showing that "most Americans tend to have little tolerance for older persons and very few reservations about harboring negative attitudes toward older people." The irony is, of course, that younger people propagate a system of prejudice that will only hurt themselves, assuming they are lucky enough to live long and grow old. We fear what we will become.

But what if our views about old people and aging are absolutely wrong? As you will see, the view from seventy and beyond turns conventional thinking about aging on its head.

The First Lesson:
Being Old Is Much Better Than You Think

Aging is one of the strangest things that happens to human beings. It's a process no one can escape, so all of humankind has at least one thing in common: we grow older. However, it is extremely difficult for most people to imagine themselves as old. The aged are mentally categorized and even treated as a different species from the young; it's as if they have always been old. We seem incapable of holding in our minds the reality of our own aging *as a process* and to develop a realistic picture of what our older selves will be like.

It's so hard for young people to imagine life in old age that researchers are looking for ways to help them do so. Psychologists Laura Carstensen and Jeremy Bailenson created an experiment to help college students envision their future selves. Using a technology called "immersive virtual reality," they made imagining an aged self more realistic. Each student looked in what appeared to be a mirror and saw a digitally age-morphed image of his or her future self. This vision of the future, the researchers found, made younger people think more realistically about things like planning for retirement. Even with such technology, however, it is remarkably difficult for the young to conceive of the reality of their lives a half century from now.

We are therefore prone to imaginings and fantasies of what late life must be like, instead of being informed by what individuals who are already there actually can tell us about it. I did ask them, and what I found profoundly surprised me. Most of the experts told me about high levels of well-being in their later years—more, in some cases, than they felt when they were younger. A new image began to replace my preconceived notions, and I found myself saying, "Being old is much better than we think it is."

Try this: Think first about your fears of the aging process and what you dread about the idea of being old. Then read these quotes a few times from people who are already there.

> Embrace it. Don't fight it. Growing older is both an attitude and a process. And if your attitude is that you're still good, you still enjoy life, there's still purpose in your life, you'll do well. (Ray Caddell, 80)

> All I would say to an eighteen-year-old is don't think of old age as old and decrepit and you're on your way to the graveyard, the morgue, or whatever. It's much better than that. There are a lot of things out there that you haven't yet experienced, and they'll bring you loads of pleasure and interest. Not the end of the road. You're still on a road that you don't see the end of yet. (Jocelyn Wilkie, 86)

> I'd tell young people that being old is great because you can do as you darn please and enjoy whatever! You're

not tied down. You can do as you want to. Take off and go someplace on your own, not being tied down and what have you. And if somebody calls you, you go. You don't stay home. Earlier in my life, if somebody asked me, no, I'd find an excuse. But now, no! I'm gone. (Ramona Olberg, 76)

The experts' basic message about aging is one of the most counterintuitive recommendations in this entire book: *don't waste your time worrying about getting old.* Old age is very different from what the experts anticipated—and it vastly exceeds their expectations. What makes being old better than most of us imagine? From the thousand elders, I learned that two things in particular make it a uniquely fulfilling time of life.

First, many experts described later life as embodying a serenity, a "lightness of being," a sense of calm and easiness in daily life that was both unexpected and somewhat difficult to describe. I saw it firsthand when I spent part of a spring afternoon with Cecile Lamkin.

A part-time helper answered the door and brought me into Cecile's living room, where a wall of windows looked out through the still-bare trees to a calm lake below. This lakeside house has been Cecile's home for over fifty years, only she'd recently given up daily swims, she said, "Because I can't get down the stairs anymore." Widowed several years earlier after sixty-eight years of marriage, Cecile explained that she remains close to her three daughters, all of whom are in their sixties. She has no illusions about her age or her time horizon, telling me with a laugh, "I'm ninety-two, so if I live to be ninety-five it'll be a miracle."

Cecile's longevity has brought limitations: "My life has become smaller since I'm older. I can't walk very well, so there are things I can no longer do easily. For example, I can't go to museums unless I'm with somebody who can wheel me around in a wheelchair. I used to go to the library all the time, but now I don't go unless I'm with somebody. I don't go shopping, so my life has become very small." But she continued: "My mind is still there. I'm a very happy person."

Like many of the oldest experts, Cecile found that later life has brought her a sense of wholeness, acceptance, and the ability to enjoy small pleasures, despite loss.

I AM MUCH CLEARER now. I say that as an older person, not just as an adult, but as an older person, things are much clearer. I was just telling my daughter, I think I'm happier now than I've ever been in my life. And I've been thinking about why it is that I'm happier now. I came up with a lot of stuff. First of all, things that were important to me are no longer important, or not as important. The second thing is, I don't feel responsible in the same way that I used to feel. I've been a pretty responsible person but I don't feel that responsibility anymore. My children are in charge of their lives, and whatever they do with them, they will do with them. And I feel pretty assured that they're okay, not that they're always going to make good decisions but that they're going to manage their lives. I also feel sure of my grandchildren. They always feel like very responsible people. I'm really proud of them.

And I live in a place, my house, that I love. In the summer here it is wonderful, and I live outdoors at that time. My family comes, friends come, and I use it like a vacation. I've also given up feeling that I have to entertain people. If there's someone coming up, they will bring such and such. It's very liberating for me. And I just feel a contentedness that I've never felt before. I've heard other people my age say the same thing.

Cecile is by no means unique. If you were to sit a representative group of my eighty- and ninety-year-old experts down in a room together, they would have one clear message to address to your nagging worry about being old: *get over it*. Because for most of them old age has been one of life's greatest surprises: a time of greater opportunity and contentment than they had ever imagined. And this feeling cut across income and ethnic groups.

My second surprise was the experts' view of *aging as a quest*. They acknowledge that growing old is uncharted territory, a transition to a world that does not have the clear road map of middle age, with its defined career ladder and child-rearing responsibilities. But many experts described it with a sense of exploring a new land, of novel opportunities to be seized and interests to be developed. Rather than a time of decline, many of America's elders see aging as an adventure.

Loraine Bauer isn't a Pollyanna. She doesn't gloss over the problems of aging; a very active and engaged person, she is irritated at age eighty-nine with the physical limitations that come with growing older. And yet she sees aging as a quest. She told me:

> THERE'S A QUOTATION FROM Tennyson's poem about Ulysses, where he says, "Come, my friends, / 'Tis not too late to seek a newer world." That has been a mantra for me my whole life. "Come, my friends, / 'Tis not too late to seek a newer world." Even if you are a hundred years old, you know?

Antoinette Watkins, when asked about what advice she'd give young people about growing older, firmly stated:

> WELL, WHAT I WOULD tell them is don't worry about it. I have found each decade, each age, has opportunities that

weren't actually there in the previous time. There've been joys in each stage of my life. The thing is—people are so afraid of getting old. Don't worry about it. It's an adventure.

For many of the experts, the adventure of old age has involved the unfolding of new opportunities and the development of new interests. Henry David, eighty-two, grew up in a family of "dirt farmers" during the Depression, living off what the family could grow to feed itself. "The Depression colored our attitudes. It colored our activities. It colored what we did. It colored what our aspirations were. It made us strive more diligently to work our way out of that Depression and do something that was better than being dirt farmers." And Henry did just that, obtaining a master's degree and working on the design of scientific instruments. He worked until he was seventy and then learned that being older can be a "blast." He says:

IN RETIREMENT I'VE BEEN able to participate in volunteer activities much more expansively than I could when I was younger, and I've enjoyed it hugely. I enjoy the opportunity to share whatever advice I might be able to offer, and you can't do that when you're twenty. You haven't built a body of experience, you haven't built your intellectual curiosity, and you can't exploit all you've learned because you haven't learned too much yet. It's in the part of life I'm in now that you can put all these pieces together and you can offer to society the benefit of what you've learned. I've had a blast for the last ten years or so. I work with historical societies and other organizations, and I have a lot of fun with it. You just are able to pull together a lot of strings that aren't available to you at twenty years of age.

I can't underscore this message enough: the time you spend as a young person worrying about aging is truly wasted, because it's likely to be much better than you expect. However, as the next lessons show, there's a lot you can do when you are younger to ensure that old age is better than you think.

The Second Lesson:
Act Now like You Will Need Your Body for a Hundred Years

One guideline for selecting the lessons for living in this book was to "avoid the obvious." For this reason I haven't focused on some commonly offered pieces of advice like "love your family" or "work hard." Similarly, most of the experts included a recommendation along the lines of "take care of your health" or "if you don't have your health, you don't have anything." In our health-conscious society—where you can't go for a single day without hearing about the dangers of trans fats, excess calories, soda, or the sedentary life—this prescription from the experts doesn't seem very newsworthy.

Except that it is. From decades of observing their own and other people's behaviors, the experts offer one profound and extraordinarily important message that can transform how you look at your health. It involves rethinking how to motivate yourself to stay healthy and how to select the habits that will be the most important in determining your experience of later life (which, remember, may last thirty years or more). Here's the core of the lesson: *it's not dying you should worry about—it's chronic disease.*

When most of us think about how our current behaviors will affect us later on, the experts say our focus is all wrong. We're thinking about death, when we should be thinking about disease.

And that leads us to make all kinds of bad decisions now that can leave us miserable years or decades later. You may not have been convinced by all those public health messages on television, or by your spouse nagging you, but I hope you will at least take the experts' advice on this one point.

Over the years, I've noticed that when people engage in a habit that's bad for their health they try to justify it by talking about dying. I give you as an example one of the people I loved most in my life: my mother-in-law. She was a five-foot-tall, feisty Scottish immigrant. She was funny, a cutthroat Scrabble player, and one of the kindest people I have ever known. But she loved bacon and sausage, red meat, Scotch whiskey, and sweets. She was also a pack-a-day smoker and not fond of exercise. I used to nag her about these health behaviors, but it fell on deaf ears.

She would tell me that she enjoyed these vices, and that she didn't care how long she lived. "People live too long anyway," she would say. She would assert that Americans worried too much about dying and that made us puritanical about health. I have had this experience over and over. Acquaintances who are obese or smokers or nonexercisers frequently say that no one lives forever and, "Well, if it just cuts a few years of my life, it's worth it to me." A devout Catholic, when my mother-in-law got fed up with me she'd tell me that her health plan was to stay in a state of grace— that way she'd be ready if she suddenly dropped dead.

And this is, according to the experts, *all wrong.* Because they know one fact firsthand: what you can expect from not making the right health decisions isn't an early death—in fact, that's the least of your worries—instead you should be concerned about years, possibly decades, of suffering from chronic disease. The smokers, overeaters, and couch potatoes among us are too focused on the comforting thought that the worst that can happen is dropping dead one day—a little earlier than other people perhaps, but who cares? The reality is that such an easy exit almost never happens. Instead we wind up with an ever-increasing burden of illness.

Let me come back to my mother-in-law. She became diabetic in her sixties—a pathway to many other health problems. As the years went on, she had a bout of breast cancer, developed emphysema, and was diagnosed with congestive heart failure. These mounting illnesses came to seem like physical weights on her, pressing her to the ground. And none of these diseases killed her (lung cancer finally did, at age eighty-two). But what she did experience was a twenty-year downhill spiral of chronic health problems. Despite a positive attitude, her experience was miserable at times, limiting her ability to socialize, travel, and enjoy daily life.

The experts agree that what you do now for your health is critically important for your future. However, the motivator should not be *how long* you live but *how* you are going to live. The person who reaches age sixty is going to live on average at least another twenty-two years. What you need to be concerned about is the quality of your life during that time. That's the message of the experts. Forget about dying (see the next lesson). You need to change your lifestyle early in life, not to live longer, but to live *better* in your seventies, eighties, and beyond. Your body may well have to serve you for a hundred years.

Todd Ouellette, age seventy-seven, put it succinctly:

WELL, I KNOW THIS: aging is okay. But if you have to be pushed around in a wheelchair with an oxygen tank, if there's anything in life that you know right now that can prevent that, do it. Because as you get older, that's when you really have an opportunity to sit back and enjoy life a lot more. But only if you're not in terrible health because you're obese or something like that. Whatever you can do to maintain your health, do it now. Stay away from cigarettes or whatever, because it will definitely make a difference later on in life.

Luisa Varga, eighty-four, agreed:

WHAT YOU DO WHEN you're young, it will hunt you up when you get old. When you're young, take care of your body, go to the doctor, and keep yourself in good shape, and don't abuse your body in any way. Too much smoking will hurt you, too much drinking, too much drugs will hurt you. So you can't overdo any of those things and that's what it takes to keep your body in shape so that when you get old your body is not hurt. Now, if you don't do that, a lot of things might come out later on in life.

These experts' point of view is backed up by sound research. Here's what's happened to the world over the past century. People used to die early of acute infectious diseases. We have overcome many of these problems through improved hygiene and nutrition, as well as medical advances. Better screening and early testing for some diseases led to lower mortality.

As the pendulum swung away from deaths due to acute illness, especially in childhood, it swung toward chronic illness. Now Americans die from heart problems, strokes, diabetes, and lung diseases. And these chronic diseases have two things in common. Unlike a death, say, from pneumonia (which my grandmother's generation called "the old man's friend" because it led to a quick and relatively painless passing), these illnesses and their effects can last years or even decades. That's why they're called chronic, after all—they go on and on.

The second thing these diseases have in common is that they are largely *preventable*. The World Health Organization makes it clear that chronic disease is primarily caused by common, modifiable risk factors. The big three? Unhealthy diet, physical inactivity, and tobacco use. This prestigious organization makes a point reinforced by the experts: everyone has to die of something, but death doesn't have to be the slow and painful process of chronic disease. And as someone who has studied the chronically ill, believe me that you want to avoid it if you can!

The saddest examples came from the experts who learned firsthand about why you should take care of yourself now. When I was in high school, we had to sit through driver's education classes, where they tried to scare us into safe driving by showing us films of gory accidents. In that spirit, let's look at a few examples of what preventable chronic disease looks like.

Daphne Pry, seventy-one, tries to remain as upbeat as possible, looking for things to enjoy in life. But the burden of caring for her chronically ill husband has taken a very serious toll. No one can say for sure whether her husband's problems were caused by not taking care of himself but all are heavily related to lifestyle.

> I DIDN'T KNOW THAT when my husband had his first heart attack and a triple bypass that was going to be the least of his illnesses, the least debilitating. Then he followed that with diabetes, which entailed diet and insulin. And then he had heart failure. And then he had a stroke. We're covering a period of about fifteen years. And talk about worrying! I wish I could figure out a way not to worry about him. Somehow I always do what has to be done. But part of me is dreading the next time.
>
> We regularly call 911, because with diabetes inevitably there are going to be times when the blood sugar goes wacky, and he's woken up three times now early in the

morning, completely out of his mind, because he was on the edge of a coma. Now the paramedics just walk in. They know the way to the bedroom.

One of the most poignant regrets comes from those who destroyed their health through smoking. The former smokers would do anything to wave a magic wand and change that one choice. Many denied the effects of smoking when they were young, assuming that the worst they could expect was an early death. Not so, as Terry Luckett, eighty-seven, told me:

TELL YOUNG PEOPLE TO choose a lifestyle as healthy as possible, both physically and mentally. I had a fairly strong constitution and I always enjoyed swimming, hiking, tennis, squash, and handball. However, I began smoking when I was in the navy in the 1940s. By the time I left business, I was consuming about three packs a day and several cigars, having stopped for almost two years and then resumed.

In 1977 I had bronchial pneumonia, in 1989 a quintuple heart bypass—after which I finally stopped smoking for good—and, nevertheless, in 1992 the removal of a malignant lung tumor. My wife smoked about half what I did and died of lung cancer. Soon after she died, following a year of radiation treatment and chemotherapy, I had aspiration pneumonia, my fourth life-threatening disease. Obviously, in addition to a healthy diet and exercise, I recommend not smoking. My only excuse is that in the early 1940s we knew less than now about addiction and the connection between smoking and heart and lung diseases. People now don't have that excuse.

Tina Oliver still mourns the loss of her husband eleven years ago.

MY HUSBAND PROMISED ME we'd have a fiftieth anniversary, and he lied to me. He left me after forty-seven and a half years. He was sick for quite a while. He had a heart attack and prior to that he had carotid surgery, first one side then the other. He was a smoker.

And not one of my children smokes, thank goodness for that. They saw how their father was. He went to the hospital, and he was there for five and a half months after he had heart surgery, and he never came back. Five and a half months. And that was fifty-two miles each day that I traveled for five and a half months, and I went every day.

But, you know, the kids saw how he had to suffer. And when you told him something about it—"Don't smoke like that"—or his drinking, he'd say, "So what? You've got to die sometime." But who suffers? The family.

The moral of the story: stop yourself when you explain poor lifestyle choices by saying something like "So what? You've got to die sometime." Because there's no guarantee of an easy way out after a life of overeating, inactivity, or smoking. The experts are telling you that you can't choose whether or not to die, but you can to some degree control whether you spend the last decades of your life in healthy productivity or in a downward spiral of physical misery.

The Third Lesson:
Don't Worry about Dying—the Experts Don't

One thing I desperately wanted to ask the experts about was death. Yes, I confess that the whole death thing has pretty much scared the daylights out of me since I became aware of it at age four or so. Other people put it out of their thoughts, but as a young person I couldn't get my mind around it—that one thing you just can't escape. Of course I'm not alone: there's even a whole school of psychological research based on the concept of "terror management." This theory (not one of the more cheerful ones in social science) posits that the awareness of our own inevitable death creates the potential for debilitating terror, against which we then find ways to psychologically defend ourselves.

If anyone should experience this kind of terror, it's the experts. They are, after all, statistically much closer to the end of life than those of us under seventy. "Time's winged chariot" is definitely "hurrying near" for each and every one of them, no matter how healthy or active they may be today. The average life expectancy in the United States is seventy-eight years, and many of my interviewees were already beyond that age. The longest scientifically verified life span (Jeanne Calment, a feisty Frenchwoman) is 122 years—a long time, if you make it that far, but still not forever.

I know it's a taboo subject, but I decided to bite the bullet and ask the experts candidly and directly about death and dying. I began with this question: "When people reach your age, they begin to realize that there are more years behind them than in front of them. What are your feelings about the end of life?" We discussed how much they thought about dying, what their expectations were, and whether death concerned them or occupied their daily thoughts.

One question repeatedly entered my mind while listening to the interviews: where's the terror? Because what the experts told me is that the intense, overpowering fear of dying is very much a young person's game. I did not detect denial from the experts but rather a matter-of-fact approach to dying and a willingness to discuss it and what it means.

The vast majority of the experts described themselves as not thinking about death often, and certainly less so than when they were younger. I was aware that research shows lower death anxiety with advancing age. Nevertheless, I wasn't prepared for the comfort level most of the experts expressed about their own deaths. Here's how some them talked about their own mortality.

Rosemary Brewster, ninety, is a regular churchgoer and has been all her life. When asked, "Do you believe in life after death?" she replied: "I often wonder about that. I think and I wonder if there really is. And I'm going to find out. I wouldn't bother worrying about it too much, because I'm going to find out." Rosemary pointed out that her feelings had changed greatly in later life.

> BUT, YOU KNOW, WHEN you're younger you go to bed and you think about death, and "Oh my God!" Or you're sick: "What if I don't wake up?" I don't think that anymore. Now that I'm old, I'm at peace when I go to bed. I figure if I don't wake up, well, maybe I'll be someplace nicer. It's just a funny thing. I used to be scared to go sleep when I wasn't feeling good, but not anymore. I'm not ready to die or anything like that, but I'm just not afraid to die. I think there's something on the other side, and I've got some sisters over there who will be waiting for me. I'm not worried at all. And that's something I didn't think I'd ever come to terms with.

We met Edwina Elbert at the beginning of this chapter. She embodied what I learned is a common attitude of the experts toward the end of life: a mix of interest, curiosity, and acceptance.

Edwina is a warm, witty, and very open ninety-four-year-old. Her brushes with a serious accident and an illness have led her to reflect on the end of life and what it means.

IT HAS MADE ME realize that there's always that question of why nobody knows where we go. Well, there must be a reason for that. We'll never know because that's a mystery. I know about as much about it as the most learned men in the world, I would imagine. Because nobody really knows what happens to you.

But I am very comfortable. I'm not afraid to die. Being near to death impacted me greatly, to be honest, and I don't talk about it. It's something that's very personal. But I'm a better person for it. I do wonder—I think God must be saving me for something and I can't figure out what it is. Maybe I'll know someday when I'm 110.

But about dying, I'm not one bit afraid. Well, if you stop to think about it, it's a natural thing. Everything dies. Whether we come back or not or what happens there, I don't know. But it's like my husband used to say whenever we did discuss it: "If you go to heaven, how wonderful. But if you go to sleep, what's wrong with that?"

As you might expect, deeply religious experts found their beliefs to be comforting as they contemplated the end of life. They often told me that they weren't worried a bit because it will be nothing more than "stepping through a door" into the next world. Typical was Marie Clarke, who at eighty-six is in poor health but doesn't worry about the end. She put it simply:

I JUST KNOW WHERE my faith is taking me and that when I leave this world I know where I'm going. The Lord's

going to call me home. And that may sound kind of lacka-
daisical and all, but this is what we're told, in his word—
that we'll be with him.

Other experts were less conventionally religious but still expressed faith in life continuing after death. Flora Turnbull, eighty,
sees death as a new beginning:

GOD HAS ALWAYS BEEN important to me. Religion and
religious practices, I've been in and out of. But spirituality,
yes. So, my thoughts about the end of life and what comes
after? A new adventure. Yes, a new adventure. I do not expect to have heaven be filled with people I'm being reunited
with. For all I know, it may be filled with people I've never
met. What an adventure that will be!

I would like to dispel the notion, however, that it's just religious people who shed an intense fear of dying as they grow older.
I found the same kind of matter-of-fact comfortableness with life's
end among experts who were vigorous nonbelievers.

Take Trudy Schoffner, for example, whom I interviewed in
her art-filled apartment in New York City. If there ever was an
urbane New York intellectual, it is Trudy. A highly self-aware,
analytical individual with a vast range of life experience, Trudy
is adamantly not religious. She told me: "I believe nature is God.
My mother and her mother came from a religious family. But my
father did not believe in religion and so we did not grow up with
religion."

Like Rosemary Brewster, however, Trudy told me about the
change in her fear of death as she aged. She explained that the
panic over death is "a younger person's game."

I MEAN, LIFE IS death and death is life. If I die, I die. Dying is what I was thinking about when I was younger. I remember thinking, "How can I die? How can I not be alive?" That panicky feeling. But now I haven't thought about it in years. I know it can't be much longer—I'm eighty-seven. But I just don't worry about it. That's why I want to go out every night, as long as I can afford it. I want to do everything I can do. But I'm not worried about dying—don't even think about it, really.

Another good example is John Starnes, age seventy-three. John grew up in a working-class home in England, the first person in his family to go to university. His interest in science began as a child and he went on to become a well-known researcher. He lost interest in religion as an adolescent:

I WAS ACTUALLY THINKING this over yesterday for some reason, to figure out when I realized I wasn't religious. I think I was around sixteen years old. I was going to church and I thought they were kind of hypocritical. I was interested in science and I was interested in philosophy. The more I learned about philosophy and science, the less I thought of religion.

John has lived his life based on reason, on healthy skepticism, and on what he considers a realistic view of the world—which excludes religious belief. This worldview did not change when he confronted life-threatening illnesses. He had a bout with cancer fifteen years ago that was successfully treated. He recently had even worse news: "Less than two years ago I was then diagnosed with multiple myeloma, which can kill you very quickly, it turns out."

So unlike many of us, John directly confronts the immediacy of death on a daily basis. Yet he remains both calm and matter-of-fact about it. When asked about his views on aging and the end of life, he told me:

> I THINK YOU HAVE to accept that you're going to grow older and you're going to die. I think if you can accept that's going to happen, it makes life easier. As an atheist I don't expect there to be an afterlife. I don't expect to go to heaven. I don't have to be afraid about going to hell. I should be very surprised if there is a hell. So I think that if you can be realistic about things it's very helpful.

Perhaps surprisingly (but like other nonreligious respondents) John believes that a realistic approach—no afterlife—is both helpful and reassuring.

Although they seem unconcerned about the fact of dying, the experts do have one end-of-life recommendation for people of all ages: *plan for it.* Indeed, when I asked many of these elders about their views of death and dying, the worry they mentioned most frequently was not being organized and leaving a load of work behind for their families. I learned that planning "for the journey," as some referred to it, was seen as responsible behavior as well as providing a significant source of comfort.

One particularly delightful interview I conducted was with Ted and Lucy Rowan. I interviewed this couple, married for fifty-seven years (as Ted put it, "to the girl of my dreams"), in their cozy apartment in a retirement community. It's an interview that I left smiling, after being treated to their warmth and companionability. Ted is a clergyman and Lucy worked in child welfare. They raised four successful children of their own and are active in the community where they live. Ted, eighty-four, still preaches when needed to fill in at local churches.

Both Ted and Lucy are by no means ready for the end. Lucy told me, "My father died at ninety-eight, my mother at eighty-nine. I'm eighty, so I feel I have at least ten more years to be productive." Ted's work has made him reflective about death, but it doesn't worry him:

EVERY ONCE IN A while I am invited to do a memorial service, and it means that I need to see how we are going to celebrate this person's life. I always try to put the emphasis not on our loss but on the celebration of that life that has been lived. I don't think a lot about my own death. I think, at least theoretically, I'm not concerned. I have the simple text from Paul's Letter to the Romans, where he says, "If we live, we live to the Lord. If we die, we die to the Lord. So whether we live or die, we are the Lord's." And that's all you really need to know.

But his approach of the end of life is *to plan*.

THE ONE THING THAT I am concerned about is that I tidy up my life so that people don't have to do it afterwards. I have boxes of papers and books. I want to be sure to tie up things having to do with wills and financial situations, to leave these things so people will know what they have to do when you're gone. And I want to do it primarily so that family doesn't have to do it, but I also want to do it for me, to tidy up things.

Lucy also finds preparing for the end of life to be comforting.

WELL, I THINK ABOUT death easily because our proxy and our will are all set. But our concern right now is more about the stuff we have. Do you see all of these things we've accumulated? Look at the albums I have, and I'm sure my children are not going to want them. What am I going to do with them? And Ted has boxes of lectures stored in a garage. I am really an organizing person, I really enjoy that.

These sentiments were echoed by many of the experts. The experience of "tidying up" one's possessions emerged as a metaphor for tidying up the loose ends of life, bringing things together in a meaningful whole rather than a disorganized set of unrelated parts. My frank and open conversations with the experts about the end of life did not reveal an underlying terror but instead curiosity, acceptance, and a desire to "prepare for the journey" ahead. And as we will see in chapter 7, the awareness of death and the short time horizon remaining produces a worldview that we all can embrace.

The Fourth Lesson:
Stay Connected

A favorite quotation of mine comes from John Rowe and Robert Kahn in their book *Successful Aging*:

HUMAN BEINGS ARE NOT meant to live solitary lives. Computer buffs would say that we are "hardwired," genetically programmed, to develop and function by interacting with others. Talking, touching, and relating to others is essential to our well-being. These facts are not unique to children or to older men and women; they apply to all of us, from birth to death.

But people differ a great deal in their social relationships as they age. Some individuals remain embedded in a stable network of social support until the end of their lives. Others manage to replace significant others they have lost with new social ties. And still others are unable to recover from loss and suffer loneliness and isolation.

Research shows that social connectedness, in the form of meaningful roles and satisfying relationships, is strongly related to psychological and physical health. The results of a famous research project known as the Alameda County Study showed that the absence of social ties predicted dying among older persons, even when taking into consideration things like social class and health status. Other studies have found that socially isolated and lonely older people are more likely to develop health problems and are less likely to engage in good health behaviors. It's very rare that social scientists agree on very much of anything, but here they do: Greater involvement in social roles and in networks of social support helps promote health and happiness in later life.

So, what's the problem? It's the fact that beginning in middle age people can struggle to remain engaged in relationships and productive roles. As we move through life, we experience critical transitions—retirement, loss of loved ones, moving from an old and familiar neighborhood—which make it more difficult to form and maintain relationships. Widowhood is also a problem: almost half of all women aged sixty-five and older are widowed. Household structure has also changed, and the percentage of older women living alone has increased greatly over time (from 24 percent in 1960 to around 40 percent today).

The experts confirmed both the critical importance of staying connected to others and the difficulties involved in doing so. Trudy Schoffner very much wishes to be active at eighty-seven. The problem, however, is that she finds it increasingly hard to find willing social partners because her friends have moved away or died:

> I LOVE THEATER AND I love jazz and cabaret. I have a lot of interests and I love to do a lot of things and I just—my big problem is that I don't have enough people to do things with in my spare time. I'd love to go out to dinner. I love to dance. I do things with a few different friends, and I belong to a theater club, but they're just not enough. I have a few friends but they're all busy. You know, I'm retired. I can do anything anytime.

Irv Kantor, seventy-seven, is younger than Trudy and married. And yet he also feels disconnected and sometimes lonely. In Irv's case life transitions have increased his isolation. He and his wife decided to leave the New York City area for a New England suburb. They made the move to be near their children and grandchildren, but Irv feels like an outsider: "I've been in New York all my life and it's a big difference. It's hard to feel connected here." Retirement also weakened his social ties: "I sort of found myself, in my middle sixties, disconnected. Not knowing where to go with my limited time that I had." But he knows it's important for him to bounce back and to seek out connections. "People my age need to stay involved with other people. It's easy to stay in your own comfort zone."

There was consensus among the experts that starting around age sixty everyone needs to be aware of the possibility of becoming isolated and take steps to stay engaged. Nicole Ambriz is very engaged in many activities. That's an intentional decision and a fundamental part of her advice about growing older:

> ALWAYS REACH OUT. YOU don't want to become isolated. And that's important for seniors. I've seen so many seniors

living in a rural area around here as I watch the neighbors grow older. When I first came, they might have been sixty or seventy, and I saw them becoming more and more isolated, and that's sad. This could happen to my husband and me. We only have the one daughter, no other relatives up here. We could easily become rocking-chair people. So I don't care what kind of hurdles you've got to jump over— you've got to keep going. As an older person, you have to be involved.

The experts agreed on two strategies in particular for staying engaged. You can use them yourselves and share them with your parents or grandparents. Here are their tips for making and keeping connections as you get older.

Tip 1: Take advantage of learning opportunities.

Being interested in the world around you and choosing to learn more about something that you are curious about stimulates the mind. Learning opportunities also have social benefits, like meeting new people, having meaningful conversations with friends and family, and sharing knowledge with others. More older adults are taking computer classes to become computer literate so they can connect with others. They use e-mail, join online support groups, and participate in chat rooms or message boards. New websites are launched almost every day that are geared toward older adults and promote information exchange about health, relationships, and retirement. And universities and senior centers offer a host of educational options for older people.

One expert in particular brought this point home to me. Arnold Schwartz is a small man who wears thick glasses and gets around with the assistance of a walker. I interviewed him in the dining room of a New York City senior center. Despite an initial appearance of frailty, there is an impish quality to Arnold, one he admittedly cultivates ("I like to kid around," he told me. "I'm very popular here!"). It was easy to forget that he is ninety-five years old. Arnold was a refugee from Hitler's Germany; his English is eloquent, spoken with the traces of a German accent. Arnold is happily married, with one son. Despite his physical limitations, he still drives, and he and his wife live independently in their own home.

I asked Arnold about the secret to his happiness.

> I WOULD SAY THAT what has helped me is curiosity. I was always very interested in people, all kinds of people. I would speak with Nazis in Germany, and communists, and Zionists. My curiosity gave me a lot throughout my life. I give computers as a good example. I was already at the end of my eighties. I didn't want to take up the computer at first, but then it gave me curiosity. I decided I didn't want to die without having learned the computer. So if somebody would ask me, even in advanced age, I would say get a computer—but it's easier if you have a grandchild who can teach you!

Throughout the interview Arnold's interest in learning about other people and his eagerness to develop new relationships shone through. He had a number of questions for me about my life and my work. As we finished he gave a sly grin and told me, "One thing I'm sorry about the interview here—that I couldn't carry out my intention of starting to interview *you*. I would have liked to see how you reacted. Next time I will ask you the questions!"

Tip 2: Make a conscious goal of staying connected.

The experts recommended that we set specific goals that will lead to greater connectedness. For example, people can decide to find out about places in their community that offer an activity they have enjoyed in the past. Further, many of the experts who maintained a large social network did so intentionally, setting schedules for themselves so they would not become isolated.

April Stern deliberately created a more active social life after the death of her husband, something she recommends to others.

I'VE LEARNED HOW IMPORTANT it is to have people in my life. And I've tried to structure my life so that I see somebody every day. I've learned to plan ahead in a way that I never did when I was part of a couple. Like, we used to love having an open weekend when we could just hang out. I don't love that now, so that if by Wednesday I see that kind of empty weekend, I work to fill it or at least to put some things in it. And I just know that that's important to me.

Similarly, Sandy Hudgens became concerned that she was becoming too isolated. She decided to take action.

I LIVE ALONE. I have two children. One lives in Georgia, the other in Texas, so I'm alone up here. We talk all the time, but I knew that I had to get out and be out with people. So I made myself a policy: accept every invitation there is. No matter what it is, just say "yes, yes, yes." It didn't matter if I didn't want to go out, I said, "Okay, I'm going to do it."

The experts recognize that staying connected can be a challenge and an active, even assertive, approach is necessary to avoid isolation. Henry David asserts that being social is something that can be learned, and it's in fact necessary to do so:

> MY LESSON IS THIS: Learn to be social. Learn to be an extrovert socially. Enjoy the people around you—don't criticize them so severely. Yes, there are pluses and minuses associated with all people, but be sociable. Enjoy their company and share what's germane in your own experience with people. They too are lonely at times and need somebody to support them. I happen to live in a county that's dominated by conservative Republicans. There are some good people among them, I'm learning [laughing]. For a liberal Democrat to say that—what heresy!

Such conscious, planned efforts to maintain contacts with friends and build new ones are not just a strategy for people the age of the experts. They recommend that we all become aware of how our networks can shrink in middle age and to take steps like these to stay connected. Remaining curious and embracing learning opportunities is one key method they recommend for continuing engagement. Equally important is actively working to stay connected, maintaining older ties and building new ones.

The Fifth Lesson:
Plan Ahead about Where You Will Live (and Your Parents Too)

You readers who are under sixty: *do not skip this lesson!* Here's why: many of you have parents (or grandparents) who are getting older and who are likely to develop care needs. And one thing we know from research is that people are highly reluctant to prepare for the future. Many older people imagine that life will just go on as it has, allowing them to live independently until they suddenly drop dead. As we saw earlier in this chapter, that's not likely to happen. People begin to experience limitations, and those who plan carefully do better over the long run. So you need to read this—if only to advise your older relatives!

Because I've done research for such a long time on the topic of families and aging, I find I'm often asked for advice about older parents. Almost invariably the question falls along these lines: "My parents are developing health problems and are more and more isolated. They live by themselves in a large house that they have difficulty taking care of. Everyone in the family knows that something tragic is going to occur, like one of them breaking a hip, and then they will be forced to move. Why won't they be reasonable and consider a move to a supported living environment?"

And I have to tell each one of them that I really don't know. I've been personally involved with relatives who have been willing to suffer with insecurity, isolation, and inconvenience to stay in their homes and who rejected any kind of senior living community even though the benefits to them would have been enormous. I've even half-jokingly considered writing a book called *Recalcitrant Parents,* based on the common feeling of adult children that parents simply won't act reasonably when called upon to plan for their futures.

Ida Munson, ninety-two, continues to lead a very active life. But she has seen firsthand that the time comes when most people cannot live well on their own. Her advice is to plan early for where you are going to live when you are older. One problem many people encounter is that they decide to make a move after they have significant health problems, which then make them ineligible for many housing options. Her point is that people benefit not only themselves, but their loved ones too, by preparing in advance.

THERE'S ONE THING IN growing older—you need to make decisions and prepare. Every stage of life is good if you prepare for it. It's when you don't prepare for the next stage of life that it becomes overwhelming. As you grow older it is especially important to choose the place where you would like to spend your later days. People wait too long to make that decision. So choose the place where you can be content and happy and where you can have whatever progressive care you need. And choose it sooner rather than later. It becomes too difficult to make the decision when you have passed a certain point.

It happened in my family. My father and stepmother were living down in Florida, and we wanted to get them into a place where they could have better care. We took them around to see a lot of places, and they said, "Oh that's lovely but not for us." But then, when they really needed it, it was too late for them to make the decision. When you wait until it's too late, somebody else has to make the decision for you and then you're not happy with it. So we chose our own place, and when we moved into a supported living community we were young enough that it became our real home. We could get into all kinds of activities and spend our life doing important things, and our kids would never have to wonder what to do with us.

I do have several hypotheses about why people won't plan ahead for a move to a more supported living situation, even when it would lead to a greatly improved lifestyle. First, there is the value of independence in American society. Many people struggle mightily to own their own home and it is a powerful symbol of autonomy. Some studies show that there is a concern about privacy and that life in a senior community will be invasive. This situation is especially true for people the experts' age, who typically went from their parents' homes into marriage and raising their own families (unlike the baby boomers, many of whom lived in group situations as young adults). All of this adds up to an unfortunate prejudice against moving from one's home to a senior living community— even though it may lead to a much better life.

There are many types of communities, ranging from entirely independent living to assisted living (where meals and services are provided). Senior living communities should not be confused with nursing homes, which now serve almost exclusively very ill and impaired people. Given the enormous range of senior living options around the country, most people can find one that meets their activity level, lifestyle, and health and social needs.

Around 150 of the experts reside in senior living communities of some kind. And, with very few exceptions, *they described the move from their home to that location as one of the best decisions of their lives.* Yes, many were reluctant initially. But they found that being in a supportive environment actually allowed them *more* freedom to engage in meaningful activities and relationships. The positive endorsement of life in senior living communities was so strong that it merits placement as one of the key lessons for aging.

The move was seen by many experts as a significant opening of opportunities, while also accommodating limitations that had developed over the course of growing old. Edward Horan, seventy-seven, and his wife found this out after a move to a retirement community:

> WE TAKE OUR MEALS in the dining room, so we're with other people at least twice a day. I didn't realize how much I missed the fun of being with people on a regular basis. Being in community with them, sharing, well, about as many activities as you're interested in. We have exercise ev-

ery morning, which is good physically and good conversation. There are small groups for different kinds of interests. There's the pool, and billiard players get together each morning, and a bridge group. I joined a writers group here, and it has been stimulating. You can find things here that are challenging socially, intellectually, physically.

Ron Hutton is another fiercely independent person who wasn't sure he'd like a senior community. He's ninety years old, raised on a "poor ranch" in western South Dakota. He worked in several careers: as a journalist, in financial management, and finally owned his own business. Ron retired in 1985 and lived many fulfilling years with his wife: "We enjoyed ourselves. We were busy with our hobbies. We traveled some." He said wistfully, "I say we kind of laughed our way through fifty-seven years. She had a good sense of humor. And I think I do too."

Ron's wife died several years ago. He began to develop serious arthritis, leading to problems with balance and mobility, and several falls. He then decided to move into a senior living community. He was initially reluctant, but moving in turned around his thinking. He looked back to an earlier life experience to show why the move is so beneficial:

I REMEMBER ONE TIME when I was selling mutual funds in a small community in Montana. There were a lot of widows in the town. And I asked the preacher one day why there were so many widows. He said, "Well, these people are ranchers. They worked hard and built a ranch. They've got all their kids involved and they turn their ranch over to the boy and they move to the town. Her work goes on, she's doing the dishes, keeping house and so on. He's got nothing to do. So he withers and dies."

So I'd say you need to get a life. Do something. Take pictures. Oh my God, have something to look forward to. I have a thing I look forward to every day. For example, I'm going to take this painting class. I've always wanted to take it. This senior community does a pretty good job. I get up in the morning sometimes feeling pretty disconnected and depressed. I get dressed, I come down to breakfast, and I don't go back depressed.

For individuals who had made the transition, this was one of their top lessons: senior living communities can be an ideal environment for older persons. Rather than representing a shrinking of autonomy and independence, such environments do precisely the opposite. If you have parents who are on the fence try showing them the examples provided here. It may nudge them toward a decision that will not only benefit them, but can also relieve their extended families of considerable uncertainty and stress.

Postscript:
Abandon the Fight against Aging

Our culture fears old age. We segregate older persons physically, just as we repress the awareness of our own aging. We do so at our own peril because most of us will live twenty, thirty, even forty years after age sixty. The experts tell us that to live a full and rich life we should instead increase our awareness of our own aging. Denial is our worst enemy: we fail to plan for later life and we pointlessly fear a negative future that may never occur. The five lessons in this chapter focus on awareness and adaptation to aging.

Here's the refrigerator list:

1. **Being old is much better than you think.** Don't waste your time worrying about getting old. It can be a time of opportunity, adventure, and growth. See it as a quest, not an end.

2. **Act now like you will need your body for a hundred years.** Stop using "I don't care how long I live" as an excuse for bad health habits. Behaviors like smoking, poor eating habits, and inactivity are less likely to kill you than to sentence you to years or decades of chronic disease.

3. **Don't worry about dying—the experts don't.** Don't spend a lot of time fretting about your own mortality. What the experts recommend is careful planning and organization for the end of life.

4. **Stay connected.** Take seriously the threat of social isolation in middle age and beyond, and make conscious efforts beginning in middle age to stay connected through new learning opportunities and relationships.

5. **Plan ahead about where you will live (and your parents too).** Don't let fears and prejudices deter you or your older relatives from considering a move to a senior living community. Such a move often opens up opportunities for better living, rather than limiting them.

Underlying these lessons is a general principle I learned from the experts: forget about the fight against aging. Unless you have been living in a bomb shelter for the past decade, you cannot have missed the barrage of advertising for "antiaging medicine." An entire subculture of quasi-medical practitioners has mushroomed up, promising to reshape your face and body and thus defeat the aging process. Cosmetic companies have joined in, pumping the airwaves full of advertising for products to make you more youthful looking.

To all of this, the experts say: *forget it!* Over and over they told me that the ultimate lesson about aging is "don't fight it." Instead they encourage all of us to accept the aging process and to adapt our activities to our changing physical abilities and circumstances. Social gerontologists have a term for this process: "selective optimization with compensation." People who age successfully select the activities they most value and optimize the returns they get from them. The compensation part means that people keep doing a favorite activity, but they adapt it so it fits with their abilities. This is a very different idea from fighting the aging process.

For Clayton Greenough, the metaphor is running:

YOU KIND OF GROW into it. You realize that if you can't be running this fast, well, you just go slower, but you keep on running. Do what you're able to do and accept that there might be some limitations. Just think of it as "well, at least I can do this much." Try to keep stretching the end of the envelope a little bit so you have an incentive to keep going as far as you can.

A number of the experts used hiking as an example of adapting to aging (indeed it seemed like both a physical and a metaphorical example). I will give the last word to the very wise Priscilla Linares, seventy-one:

I'VE ALWAYS BEEN A big hiker. About five years ago, I was up in the Adirondacks hiking my most beloved mountain. Four friends and I go there. We're from all over the country and we meet up there. We can't do what we used to do, but we still plod around up there.

But about five years ago, I was diagnosed with heart issues. I started not being able go up big mountains anymore. That mountain was one of them. I tried to get up it in the way I always have, loving and excited. But I could not get to the top. I had to stop. I was so upset and angry. I sent my friends on ahead and I came back down, crying and mad. I packed my gear up and came back home.

Finally, after some time and thinking about what was going on, I saw my options: to not accept what was going on for me and be mad all the time or to figure out other ways I could still be up in the mountains. I had to learn to accommodate. So I go back every year. I hike the ones I can. They're not the very tall ones anymore, but I'm not too young anymore.

The experts never give up. They run, they climb, and instead of fighting aging with gimmicks and expensive medical procedures, they accept and adapt. It's an approach that leads to fulfillment instead of frustration, and it's something everyone who is aging (that's all of us) should learn.

CHAPTER 6

❖ ❖ ❖

I Can Look Everyone in the Eye

Lessons for Living a Life without Regrets

Gertrude Towers, 76

REMEMBER, YOU ONLY GET one chance to go through this life. Don't ruin it for yourself by doing something foolish. Be safe. Be careful. What you do now, you will always remember. You'll always feel joy or regret about it happening. A friend who was going to a high school reunion told me, "The best part is I can look every single one of the other people there in the eye and be proud, and not have regrets or be embarrassed." Think about that when you start to do something you might regret.

THE LEGENDARY FRENCH CHANTEUSE Edith Piaf made famous the song "Non, je ne regrette rien." In it she claims that she regrets nothing at all because everything in her life is "paid, wiped away, or forgotten." It would be wonderful indeed to have this attitude, but most of us experience regrets as we make our way through life. Common regrets are about small, day-to-day sorts of things. We wish we hadn't eaten that third Italian sausage, hadn't snapped unkindly at a coworker, or had remembered to change the oil before the engine started smoking. We suffer from buyer's remorse: I made the mistake of going shopping for a car with my teenage daughters and came home with a sporty-looking but uncomfortable and unreliable gas-guzzler. These kinds of second thoughts happen all the time and we generally brush them off after moping for a while.

But people can also be haunted for a lifetime by decisions made decades earlier. Some of the most poignant and evocative movies feature characters who are magically allowed a second chance to right a wrong or to say what was left unsaid—as evidenced by the tears shed over films like *Ghost* and *The Sixth Sense*. Major regrets are particularly acute because we feel so powerless about them—unlike in Hollywood portrayals, no time machine will allow us to return and change the past. Even with the passage of many years it can be difficult to come to terms with remorse for opportunities missed, harmful actions, or crucial words left unsaid. No one has put it better than the poet John Greenleaf Whittier: "For of all sad words of tongue or pen, the saddest are these: 'It might have been!'"

Most of us would prefer a life with few regrets. If we knew how, we would almost certainly focus our choices and behaviors so as not to rue them when it's too late. After listening to a thousand older people reflect on their lives, I came away firmly believing that even if we can't eliminate regret, younger people *can* take steps to ensure that regrets are few and far between.

Based on their eighty thousand or so years of combined life experience, the experts are reliable guides to what you are likely to regret or feel proud of. In the interviews I was particularly interested in learning something very specific: what are concrete things younger people can do now to avoid regrets in later life? From hundreds of hours of interviews, I was able to extract five core lessons for living a regret-free life. The awareness of what the oldest Americans believe to be the most significant regrets, and how to prevent them, can help you in making decisions today and to avoid saying in your later years, "It might have been!"

The First Lesson: Always Be Honest

I apologize in advance for sounding like I'm preaching to you. But I hope that you will give me special permission to do so, because I'm not preaching from my own experience and point of view. The elders who contributed to this book offered one prescription for regret-free living so unanimously (and so vehemently) that I'm going to preach to you on their behalf. In connection with avoiding later-life remorse, one word was repeated again and again: "honesty."

This virtue is deeply rooted in the elders' worldview, so much so that it appeared to most of them to be self-explanatory. The experts were asked, "What are the major values or principles you live by?" Just about everyone included a response like "Always be honest" or "Honesty" or "Tell the truth and don't cheat anybody." For people age seventy and beyond, honesty is an indisputable core value, one that was bred in the bone when they were children. But it's also the key to a practical lesson—one that many of them have learned the hard way—for avoiding regret.

A typical response came from Arnie Hoffman, eighty-three, who gave this advice:

> HONESTY IS THE ONE value that will guide you through the rest of your life. I think honesty controls everything. If you're honest with yourself, you'll be honest with your wife and family. If you're honest with all the people around you, no matter what happens, you can look at yourself in the mirror in the morning and say, "I haven't done anything wrong." In other words, you've made the right decision if you're honest.

In their views on honesty, the experts didn't leave much wriggle room. Yes, some suggested that a "little white lie" might occasionally be okay (for example, when dealing with no-win questions like "Do these pants make me look fat?"). However, with a consistency that surprised me, they advise us unconditionally to be honest, to have integrity, to be someone others can trust. If not, we will regret it. The prescription to be honest was usually unqualified. I didn't hear, "Be honest when you have to," or "Be honest up to a point." Instead America's elders saw this prescription as unconditional: *be honest above all*. Arthur Moffatt, eighty-six, learned this lesson through the example of his father:

> IT'S AN ABSOLUTE FUNDAMENTAL: honesty is the best policy. My dad had a clothing store and as you walked down Main Street you could see the sign: "Just one price—one just price." So simple, but it says it all. In other words they

dealt fairly and squarely with the people that came in the door. In some stores, if the person was a stranger, the stranger was given a long price and the next person, who was a friend, that person was given a short price. Nothing like that—everyone was treated the same. So those are absolute basics if you want to simplify life and keep yourself out of traps and pitfalls. "Just one price—one just price." You deal with everybody fair and square.

"Fair and square" is not an expression we use much anymore, but it is a very important one to people the age of the experts. They grew up with the idea of a "square deal"—the phrase comes from the idea of a true square in carpentry, with no funny angles. You feel good about yourself, they argue, when you treat others fairly and honestly. And when people violate this ironclad rule, the experts told me, *they regret it*. Perhaps not immediately, but our elders assured me that when you get to the eighth decade of life and beyond, you will look back and rue both your own acts of dishonesty and those that were done to you. The legacy of dishonesty, I learned, has a long reach.

One discussion of honesty made a particular impression on me. It was at the end of a long day of interviews, and the late afternoon sun slanted through the windows of Eugene Earnhart's room in an assisted-living facility. Eugene is a trim, handsome man with close-cropped gray hair. He looks a decade younger than his eighty years, despite his health problems. Eugene's speech is halting due to the effects of a stroke, and it took him a while to tell me his most important life lesson. He did so with such emotion that he was forced to stop at times to collect himself before continuing. But in the end, he was relieved at the knowledge that others might profit from his experience.

Eugene served in the Korean War and later worked in manufacturing. His career involved frequent relocation and extensive business travel. The traveling was bound up with a life regret he cannot get over. He told me:

> LISTEN, THIS IS VERY important and it's . . . it's that people should respect fidelity. I'm the worst one in the world to appreciate that because I was not a faithful husband and I regret it. I think it was the fact that I roamed around the country in my work. And I really want to make this point about how fidelity is important to marriage. That's what I'd do over if you could. Oh, definitely! I was an idiot.
>
> And she was a wonderful wife. I could never make it up to her. Even to the end, I was unfaithful. Fidelity wasn't there. It's hard for me to say this and sometimes I get really depressed about it. But tell people, "Don't ramble around the country, doing what I did." Faithfulness is one of the most important things that people should cling to.

The same principle holds for honesty in the workplace. Larry Handley experienced betrayal in his job. A dishonest superior plotted to have him laid off because he wished to distribute Larry's sales territory to other employees. Decades later, this experience is still painful. "You know, you experience things from somebody that you believed in and trusted, and you find out that they did something exactly the opposite of what they told you." This betrayal made him all the more dedicated to honesty at work, and he found satisfaction—even, he says, joy—in treating others honestly:

> IN YOUR LIFE AND your work the important thing is being honest and truthful. Don't give any kind of baloney to your customers. You just level with them. There were times when I had customers that thought they wanted to buy

something, and I said, "Well, I don't know if that one would fit in for you here." Can you imagine—I would be turning down more business! But it always works out. I emphasize to my nephews and nieces and everyone, as you lead your life always be honest and truthful. Always. Then you'll never have to worry about something being found out and people thinking less of you. You can be at peace knowing you've told the truth. It's a joyful thing, really.

Particularly regretful are those who themselves bent the rules at work. Some experts admitted that they had failed to be honest in their jobs and they paid a heavy psychological price. Jordan Wiser is a good example.

I interviewed Jordan in the large and comfortable living room of a restored farmhouse in New England. We sipped coffee while looking out through a picture window onto the early spring land-scape. Jordan, seventy-seven, is the quintessential self-made man. He grew up in Brooklyn, dropped out of high school to join the service, and later became a successful entrepreneur. Like many of the businesspeople I interviewed, he noted that the temptation to bend the rules to earn larger profits is always present. And he was tempted himself, but his one brush with the "shady side" of business cured him forever and made the importance of honesty his most important life lesson.

I'LL TELL YOU WHAT it was so you understand. I was involved with an import business. So we were tempted to do something shady. We couldn't bring the items directly into the States because the duty rate was much higher, so we shipped to a different country and they put their labels on them, this country, and then the duty rate was much less and then they shipped it directly to the States. So it was lying. Of course U.S. Customs got wind of it and became interested. Yep, we got through it, but I was very lucky. It wasn't on a grand scale, and it was not crooked exactly, but it was skirting the law and you can't do those things.

Since then I will not even go near anything like that. It's not worth it. You absolutely don't want to be getting up in the middle of the night saying, "What happens if this happens, if that happens?" Believe me, it's not worth it for money to do questionable stuff. It will destroy you.

If one lets the imagination roam, there are hundreds of possible values and principles that could be held up to create a regret-free life. Think of the Boy Scout law: loyal, helpful, friendly, cheerful, thrifty, and so on. And yet from the enormous list of possible virtues to recommend, one in particular was mentioned over and over: *always be honest*. It's up to you, but if you choose to ignore it, don't say they didn't warn you!

The Second Lesson:
Say Yes to Opportunities

We've all met people who conceive of their lives in the narrowest possible terms. They are firmly stuck in their niches, walled in by an office or cubicle, and determined to stay in a comfort zone of limited range. I've seen people who turned down a promotion for fear it would be too time-consuming or taxing, or who rejected a chance to spend a year or two abroad because they were "not the adventurous type," or who avoided the opportunity to make a public presentation because it made them nervous or would be too much trouble. People become trapped by their own conception of their limits, such that they come to resent even being asked to step beyond them.

The experts' view? This approach to life is a huge mistake. Their advice is to embrace new challenges at every turn, saying yes as often as possible. The most frequently reported regrets about work in particular involved times when opportunity knocked and they kept the door firmly closed. According to our elders, the greatest reward you can receive in your career is the opportunity to do more.

Joe Schlueter, seventy-three, brought home this lesson to me. Joe began his life, like many other children of the Depression era, living in poverty. His father worked in textile mills and never finished high school. Joe's childhood engendered in him a strong work ethic and a good head for finances. After attending an Ivy League school (not bad for the first person in his family to go to college), he became an engineer and entrepreneur, involved in corporate leadership positions throughout his career. In his sixties he became the leader of a business incubator and then finally moved to a job as a lecturer at a prestigious university, teaching M.B.A. students about entrepreneurship.

So here we have a genuinely knowledgeable source: someone who came from little, succeeded as an entrepreneur, and translated his life experience into training for elite business students. His most important lesson? *Say yes.*

THE LESSON I LEARNED is that it really pays to say yes, unless you've got a really solid reason to say no. And in my work life I didn't say no. I agreed to do things. It wasn't all fun, all the time, but it often led to something interesting. The opportunities come and if you say yes, you don't do too much twice.

This principle is true with work, with volunteering, and all kinds of things where people say, "You want to do this?" Well, why not? Life gets boring if you say, "No, I don't want to try anything new." And people shouldn't be held back because they don't think they are qualified. I can think of any number of things I didn't think I was qualified to do, but if somebody else does, take their word for it and give it a go. You can learn. Or compensate for it in lots of ways.

So if you're one of these people that says, "No, I can't do that," or "I don't want to do that," you're missing a lot of what life has to offer. Life is an adventure, but to take advantage of it you have to say yes to things.

According to the experts, most people encounter turning points at which they have a clear choice. This choice is not, as you might think, "should I stay or should I go?" It is often a decision about doing something new on the job: a training opportunity, an offer to take on new responsibilities, the chance to move into a new area with which one is unfamiliar. There are a host of possibilities, but the experts concur on this one point: *say yes*. As far as work is concerned, those experts who were happiest about their careers can point to a decision where they were tempted to say no, where staying the course was more comfortable and less risky, but they finally decided to give it a go.

Shelley Donaldson worked her way up to directing a large social service program. She endorsed the idea of saying yes to opportunities, even if it seems risky.

YOU MUST BE OPEN to new opportunities. I can remember when I moved on from my first job. A person at another agency said to me, "Why don't you apply for this position?" And I said "Because your job description asks for five years' experience." I just didn't think I could do it and I was going to say no. I remember him saying, "Well, we'll take care of that." I was given the opportunity to interview and got the job. If you're so risk adverse, you're not going to get those new opportunities.

It's not often that someone presented a lesson in the form of a poem, but Albert Folsom, who we've heard from before, was full of surprises. He spent his career as a farmer who created several successful spin-off businesses. He suffered numerous setbacks on the way to success, not from the layoffs or downsizing that threaten corporate workers, but rather from perils that plague farmers: disastrous weather and fire. Reflecting on his experiences from the vantage point of a comfortable semiretirement, he related:

> I HAVE HAD A terrific life, a lot of good luck and good health. But as far as any earth-shaking advice, well, I do have one thing. One night I didn't sleep well and I dreamt. When I woke up in the morning, I wrote a poem. I don't consider myself a poet, but I wrote this and made a copy for each one of the grandchildren. Let me read it to you.

He took a breath and read it aloud. Here's part of his poem:

> What do I say if you ask me, "Grandpa,
> Where do I go from here?"
> Will I tell you the fun, of a race well run,
> Or the trouble, the pain, and the fear?
> Will you have the courage to take what life hands you,
> The trials, the troubles, the sweat?
> And then when the cards are stacked against you,
> To come back and double the bet?

Albert then explained:

HERE'S WHERE THAT CAME from. My father used to play cards, a little Monday-night poker. He quite often won. I said, "How did you win?" He said, "Well, when I lose I double the bet." My wife and I have followed that advice. One night we woke up, the sky was red. Our shed was on fire. We lost our entire packing shed and the ends of some of the greenhouses. So we cleaned up the mess, and when I rebuilt I made it twice as long as it was before. My father showed up and said, "What are you doing?" I said, "Well, you told me to double the bet!"

That's what we've always done. We were wiped out by hail one time. I mean, it took every pane of glass. We came back and rebuilt, and built larger and more. And one winter we had unusually heavy wet snow. In the morning our greenhouses were crushed flat. There was nothing left. So we built more and we built bigger. That's what I was trying to get across in what I wrote. Anyhow, I'm a little bit embarrassed to read my poem, but it kind of sums up the way we've run our lives.

My interviews make clear that the experts who took a risk at a crucial juncture were those who looked back with the greatest satisfaction on their work lives. For many of the most successful elders, the "say yes" attitude formed their core approach to work. For others, missed opportunities proved a serious source of regret near the end of their lives.

This is the existential dilemma we all face. We cannot take two paths at once. At some point we must decide, and as far as our life's work goes, not deciding is in fact a decision. The poet Robert Frost portrays such a choice in his beautiful image of a traveler forced to decide when "two roads diverged in a yellow wood." Like Frost's traveler, we ultimately must choose a path and take the consequences: "I took the one less traveled by, / And that has made all the difference."

I thought of this poem when I considered the contrast between two particular interviews. The juxtaposition of the lives of the two individuals brought into sharp focus the consequences of saying yes or no to opportunity. One path involved risk and led to fulfillment; the other was cautious and led to regret.

There is much in common between Rod Harrison and Vincent Morris. Both live in major East Coast cities. They are men of remarkably similar backgrounds, are only few years apart in age, and both had long marriages. They attended prestigious universities and had a strong interest in the arts (Rod in music, Vincent in writing). However, in the 1950s both men found themselves stuck in midlevel jobs in business. I learned an important lesson from Rod, who offered advice to younger people about work based on what he did *not* do. The contrast to Vincent's life story is striking. One said no, the other said yes, and it made all the difference.

Rod is an active eighty-year-old with a number of interests, but I noticed a touch of sadness about him when he discussed his work life, as if something had never quite clicked.

I SPENT MY ENTIRE career at the same company. Early on I decided I would always leave work on time. I had a moment when this became clear to me. They gave out awards for how long you had been employed—every five, ten, fifteen, twenty, twenty-five years you got an award for being a veteran. And when I was there in my first year, a veteran executive came by to celebrate the thirtieth anniversary of the office manager. And the office manager hobbled out of his office with a cane. The executive himself looked terrible, and somebody said, "Oh, he just had a heart attack a few months ago."

And then another long-term executive walked out of the office next to his, and he also looked in terrible physical shape. And I thought, "My God, this business can be damaging to your health." I decided then and there that I was not going to let that happen to me. I left every day pretty much when I was supposed to, and I didn't bother to hang around at night to impress anybody.

Despite the lack of commitment, Rod became a manager and was relatively successful, which allowed him to save enough to retire early. Although pleased with his good retirement package, Rod regrets that his work life stayed at a plateau and that he never felt passion and purpose in his job.

IF I HAD TO do it over again, I certainly wouldn't have gone to that corporation. At that company I never really believed in myself. I never really believed that I was better than the people I was working with. And you can't do that in a company that is so based on fierce dog-eat-dog competition. I would not take initiative—stand up for what I wanted. I would never do that, you know. I would allow myself to be somewhat intimidated. I would say to young people entering the workforce, "Stand up and shout." I didn't do that. I was much too retiring. I think you have to be not so hard on yourself, and I was really hard on myself.

Despite the money that I have now from that job, I would probably do it differently. Music is more important to me than anything else. And I would have liked to be, not so much an actor or a musician—probably couldn't have been a conductor, maybe so, I don't know—but I would have loved to have been in the business of putting music in front of the public. I would have loved to have been involved in the arts at that level.

Shortly after I spoke with Rod, I interviewed Vincent, age seventy-seven. Some of the experts took time to open up, sharing their advice in halting fits and starts. Not Vincent, from whom a carefully considered philosophy for living emerged in a flow of complete and well-crafted sentences. I met with him in his book-lined apartment on New York's Upper East Side. Vincent is very positive about old age and what it has brought him: "You are freer," he says, "than you can ever imagine yourself being."

The path of Vincent's career stands in clear contrast to that taken by Rod. As I pointed out earlier, the two men had much in common in terms of background and original career choice. But Vincent experienced a turning point where, in one moment, he said yes.

IF YOU'RE LUCKY, AND I've been very lucky, you find a vocation that is as much like what you adore as you can make it. At thirty-two I decided to abandon a not very successful career as a businessman and pick a much more successful career as a writer. And the change has been very wonderful because I earn a living with what I would do for fun. Very, very few people have the opportunity to do that. You've got to try to do that.

But Vincent nearly wound up with a career in business, instead of a profoundly fulfilling life as a writer. He likes a good plot twist, and for him the decision hinged on one particular moment in his life.

MY WIFE WILL DENY it to her dying day, but it's her fault. We were sitting on the beach. We had a kid and another one, I think, on the way. And I said to her, with the waves coming in, in that very poetic environment, "Well, I really want to be a writer. I was educated to be one as an English major. I've always wanted to be one, and now I'd really like to try to be that which I want to be." And I said, "I waited this late in life, thirty-two, to make a decision like that. I know I need credentials. I'll work for a magazine. It might be beans and bread for a long time, maybe forever. But, you know, I don't want to get to be forty and look back over my shoulder and say, 'If I'd only really had the strength of character to change.'" And Laura said to me, "What took you so long to make up your mind?" And then I knew that the young girl I met many years before, and was lucky enough to fall in love with and marry, was really a distinguished person and a brave woman in her own right.

Vincent went on to a successful career as an author; he's written biographies, stories, speeches, "Anything where people want you to put ideas into words, that's what I write. I've been doing this for a long time. I still enjoy taking a white sheet of paper and filling that thing up. That's interesting." His lesson: avoid getting stuck doing something you're not passionate about.

PEOPLE IN THEIR TWENTIES and thirties get stuck in professions they don't like because the material rewards are so great. By the time you get to be forty or fifty, I think some of the brighter ones are having second thoughts. I believe you need to think beyond yourself and your material concerns. I call it the "little man syndrome." You go up and you sit on the beach and the water washes in and washes out and it says, "Little man, what happened to you? Look up, the Big Dipper doesn't care how much money you made working for JP Morgan. It just doesn't matter."

I was deeply affected by these two interviews, forming as they do a mirror image: two paths, two choices. One leads to the sense of a life fulfilled, and the other to a sense of what might have been. The key difference was saying yes at the right moment and being willing to take the risk and the financial consequences of that decision.

The Third Lesson:
Travel More

In every interview, I asked the experts to talk about their childhoods—where they were raised and what life was like for them. Listening to the accounts of their early experiences, I was struck by how *local* they were. They were raised in different parts of the country and in different cultural milieus, but most of them shared one thing: their childhood worlds were small, stable, and firmly located in a particular place. Those from rural America might well have spent their first eighteen years without (or only rarely) leaving the county they lived in. The same was true for the urbanites—neighborhoods formed the boundaries of their lives. In fact, for some experts venturing from the Polish neighborhood where they lived to a restaurant in the Italian section counted as an exotic trip! As one ninety-year-old told me, "If you grew up in rural Kansas like I did, all the people you ever knew were from rural Kansas."

For many of the men, everything changed in World War II, when they were sent to far-flung places they knew only from the schoolroom globe: France, North Africa, Australia, Hawaii. Sail-

ors visited ports that seemed like something out of a fairy tale.
Over and over, men now in their eighties and nineties shook their
heads in amazement as they recalled what it felt like to be abruptly
removed from rural Texas, small-town Minnesota, or a working-
class neighborhood on Staten Island and shipped all over the
world.

Zack Danko, eighty-seven, spoke with that kind of wonder:

I SERVED IN WORLD War II. You traveled the world and
you bumped into people that were quite different. I was in
the Pacific, so I was talking to natives in New Guinea.
When I was younger, I would have shied away from them.
You couldn't speak the language, number one. Everything
was sort of hand movement—you try to describe what
you're trying to say. But they were the most beautiful people
in the world, what they did for us. So you look back at that,
and it teaches you things. It is a big world.

After the war, the world looked bigger to men and women
alike. The advent of television brought images of foreign countries
into people's homes and more easily accessible plane travel made
international trips possible for the middle class (remember that
even by 1960 only a small percentage of the population had ever
flown in an airplane). For some of the experts, travel became a passion and they explored the United States and the rest of the world.
For others, trips were short and relatively few. But I learned that
whether they had visited dozens of countries or stayed put in one
place, the experts had one thing in common: *they wished they had
traveled more.*

I came away from my interviews with the realization of the
profound meaning travel has at the end of life. To sum up what I
learned in a sentence: when your traveling days are over, you will

wish you had taken one more trip. Often, after a long narrative about trips taken, I heard an elder say wistfully, "But I always wish I'd visited . . ."

The award for the most avid traveler among the experts goes to Lee Farrier, who is only slowing down a bit at age ninety-seven. Lee began a lifetime of travel as a young man in the 1930s, when he embarked on his first trip around the world. He spent a half year circling the globe on his own, when travel wasn't easy. "So I've had a lot of adventures. And I was in a great many dangerous situations. I almost lost my life several times in interior China. And I think one of the things I learned is to take chances, reasonable chances, that is. You have to be a little bit adventurous." Lee's wife of sixty-five years has an adventurous spirit as well—she accompanied him on four more round-the-world trips, at one point being airlifted out after an accident on a trek in Latin America. Although he didn't precisely say his traveling days are over, Lee allows that he's developed a little trouble walking. But no one—even a world traveler like Lee—is satisfied: "There are a places I wish I'd seen, places I'd still like to go."

The experts have a special message for younger people regarding travel: *do it now.* According to Ruth Helm, some of the most regretful elders she knows are those who put off travel until it was too late—a mistake she almost made, had it not been for her husband.

MY HUSBAND TAUGHT ME that lesson because he loved to travel, but I wasn't into it so much. I was reluctant. I said "Let's wait till we're older." But he stuck to it. He told me, "No, let's travel now. Who knows if we can go when we're older?" So we traveled all over the world, almost. We did Europe. We did Asia. Oh, I loved it. It's true, you could get sick, you could die—so go now. If you can, without hurting your financial or social or family life, do as much traveling as possible while you are young

Marcela Youssef, seventy-six, is another expert who is end-lessly grateful that she took trips while she could. She had few op-portunities to travel as a young person, and after marriage she remained near her home town. Because of her husband's new job, even a honeymoon trip wasn't possible. Through careful planning, however, the couple more than made up for that when they took early retirement.

> THESE PEOPLE THAT DON'T retire, that continue to work until they're so exhausted, don't make any sense. My husband and I both retired in our fifties. We wanted to travel. And we have literally been to every state and every province in the U.S. and Canada and to Europe too. After the children got out of college, we carefully saved our money so that we could travel. And we traveled as long as we could until eventually my husband became ill and we couldn't travel anymore. I am so glad we did it while we could! We loved every minute of it, and because we did our traveling, I have no regrets.

So here's a clear opportunity to avoid a future regret: travel while you have the time and the physical ability, and while you can have your favorite travel companion by your side. This message comes from some of the experts who delayed travel until it was too late. In most of Bettina Grover's long interview, the happy eighty-six-year-old expressed no complaints or regrets. But she had spent her life close to home, and it was with a very wistful look in her eyes that she told me simply, "I always wanted to go to Hawaii, but I never made it. Oh, it's too late for me."

Jack Baltar, eighty-one, lost his wife, Lynne, to cancer after they retired. He did some traveling on his own, but he realized that he had waited until it was too late:

> WE ALWAYS THOUGHT WE'D do a lot of lot of traveling when we retired, you know? But then Lynne passed away, and it was too late. I went on a couple of trips and I guess they were okay, but it's less fun going alone. I took a bus through the Canadian Rockies, and I actually turned once to talk to her—I was sitting in a seat by myself and it was beautiful, and I wanted to tell Lynne, "Look at that light, the color, that light." But of course she wasn't there. And I just want to share things with her when I travel, but we waited too long.

I can hear some of you saying, "That's all well and good, but how can we afford it?" The experts counter by saying that travel is so rewarding that it should take precedence over other things younger people spend money on. They believe travel has special benefits for the young because it broadens their horizons, helps them to find a focus for their lives, and challenges them in new ways. Donna Loflin, seventy-eight, summed up the experts' priorities regarding travel as follows: "If you have to make a decision whether you want to remodel your kitchen or take a trip—well, I say, choose the trip! And travel when you're young because your health allows you to do things that you can't do when you get older. Material things, you can wait on those."

Of course travel is by no means only for the young—although the experts do realistically note that the older you get, the more difficult it is to withstand the rigors of travel. The importance of travel is highlighted by the extraordinary lengths to which some experts go to keep seeing the world well into old age. Travel is just that important to feeling, at the end, like your life has been well lived.

Donna Loflin shows this kind of determination. "Travel is so important. I still travel, even though I am prone to falling. I fell in Russia. I fell in Italy." She laughed. "A friend wants me to go to Germany. Well, I'm willing to fall in Germany if it's necessary!"

Rosemary Brewster felt so strongly about the importance of travel that she made nearly heroic efforts so she and her husband could take the trips they loved. He was very ill, but that didn't stop them. She told me, "Hey, he was on dialysis for eight years, and we didn't stop traveling. I just turned my nights into days." I wanted to hear more about this.

> I GOT UP IN the night to do the dialysis because you don't want to do it on the road. We went out to Saskatchewan. We went to British Columbia. We traveled to New Orleans. We went all over the States because I could have his stuff sent anywhere in the States. It was difficult, but we traveled because we wanted to be together and he didn't to miss out on everything just because he got sick. And we had saved our money for traveling, so we weren't going to miss out on it. We set up our I.V. pole and everything. When we went on bus trips, when everybody got off the bus we shut it down and exchanged it. We were able to go anyplace in the States or Canada.

Any excuse you have for not traveling probably pales by comparison to these examples. So make a list of the places you would like to see and the trips you want to take. Then match it up against the years you expect to able to travel comfortably (if you are the exception, it may be ninety; if you are closer to the rule, for anything other than bus tours, say eighty). You may get lucky, but why take chances? Put a plan in place for how you are going to get there while you still can. Because from the expert point of view, when people reach the last decades of the life span, they are very likely to regret not having traveled more. This is one case where "Don't put off until tomorrow what you can do today" should be your motto.

The Fourth Lesson: Choose a Mate with Extreme Care

Out of millions of eligible partners in the world, most of us wind up committed to one particular person with whom we have decided to spend our lives. Somewhat miraculous, isn't it? For an avid reader, like me, of the *New York Times* wedding pages, the pathways to "I do" seem as diverse as the couples themselves. People meet through work, through play, in bars, on blind dates, at class reunions, and increasingly over the Internet. The fact that most of us do discover one special individual out of an enormous set of possibilities lends a feeling of destiny to what social scientists blandly call "the mate selection process."

The experts agree on one thing: this is probably the most important decision a human being makes. And yet, looking back over their own experience and observing many others, their view is that we are *not careful enough*. They assert that people tend to do one of three risky and possibly disastrous things. First, they can fall passionately in love and commit immediately, Romeo-and-Juliet-style (and look how that turned out). Second, they can (especially as they reach their midthirties) commit out of desperation, for fear that no one better will come along. Third, they can drift or fall into marriage without the choice or its reasons ever becoming clear. (I played poker with a guy who announced unenthusiastically during a game that he was marrying his girlfriend because, well, it seemed like about time to do it. Good thing he was pretty skilled at bluffing!)

The experts vigorously reject these pathways to marriage. Whether it is an impulsive move, a perceived last-chance leap, or a slide into the inevitable, their advice is to stop, look, and listen. Question the decision, then question it again. Or you may be in for deep and serious regrets.

Some very strong testimony in favor of waiting and choosing carefully comes, as you might predict, from experts who experienced failed marriages. Quite a few of these individuals married a second time and had the satisfaction of "getting it right" after an initial fiasco. These elders typically attributed the failure of the marriage to not making the time and effort to gain a deep knowledge of their partner before marrying. This is what they urge the rest of us to avoid: marrying the wrong person. As Phyllis Morton, seventy-eight, said bluntly: "It is better to not marry than to marry the wrong person. Both my husband and I were married once before and it took that experience to learn this lesson. We both learned it, and we're happy now."

Keith Koon advises:

DON'T RUSH IN WITHOUT knowing each other deeply. There is a typical trap when young people get into marriages. When you are in the romantic phase, you want to be on your best behavior all the time, so we say what we think the other wants to hear. It's very dangerous, but people do it all the time.

The potential danger of the "romantic phase" was a frequent cautionary note struck by the experts. As Sarah Palmer, eighty-four, another divorced but happily remarried expert, put it:

WELL, PEOPLE AREN'T ALWAYS what they seem. It's very
bad if you don't really know them until after you marry
them. My husband, I thought he wanted the same things I
did and I found out he didn't have any idea what I wanted
and I really didn't have any idea what he wanted. And the
things we wanted were totally and completely different, like
night and day. That was a rather large, large error, but I was
so in love with him that I couldn't see anything else, and
that's a big problem.

Henry David responded without hesitation to the question
about how to have a happy marriage: *choose carefully*. He told me
that taking additional time is something of an insurance policy
against later regret:

I THINK THE INJUNCTION that I'd like to offer to young
people is this: be very, very careful about the selection of a
life partner and look well beyond the near horizon and as
far into the future as you can. Realize that there are going
to be challenges through your life and this person you're
considering is the one you'd like to have with you as you
face future problems. I didn't do very well and I'd like to
pass that advice along to young folks. Look for a life partner
very carefully, even rejecting some that you think might be
very good. But of course do it diplomatically!

Kate de Jong was eager to talk about the many ways in which
her life is delightful. For one thing, she loves the midwestern town
in which she resides: "I love this place! It's absolutely the greatest
place I could ever imagine." At seventy-five, she has a fulfilling
social life. "I've been blessed with dear friends and good health.

Those are all things that contribute to my well-being certainly. And I am inclined to give back as much as I can. I love to volunteer just because I know I can do it as a gift of myself."

As the interview progressed, however, Kate opened up about her one major regret: not choosing the man she married more carefully, a decision that has cast a shadow over her adult life. Kate's parents were divorced when she was a young child, which was highly unusual when she was growing up in the early 1940s. "There weren't divorces. My mother lived with quite a humiliating and embittered feeling. Although she didn't show it much, I know that she was very, very upset by it." An important part of Kate's story stems from that childhood experience: she was bound and determined not to get divorced herself.

Unfortunately, however, she chose the wrong person, a decision that has haunted her ever since. Kate has found a way of accommodating, but only by working around an unhappy marriage for fifty years.

> AS FAR AS MY own outlook on the marriage, I'd say it's been a rough, rough passage, in part because of my sheer determination to stick it out. I did not want to go through a divorce. My husband lives very much on his own track. And I don't seem to have much of a part in his life. So I've developed a life of my own. We cohabit, but I would not call our relationship a good marriage at all. Communication is the biggest barrier, I think. I'm a talker. He's not. He can't express his feelings. Why, I don't know. I never have. I never will, probably.

Kate's message is clear: taking the time to know someone before marriage can prevent years, or even decades, of difficulty as life goes on. So whether you are a young person embarking on a first marriage or someone in middle age thinking of the "second time around," you have a golden opportunity for regret prevention. As Jeff Baylor, ninety-one, told me: "When you think you've found your true life partner, think twice, three times, or however many times it takes before you take the step into marriage. Investigate it more thoroughly than any other decision, weigh your options, and in particular examine your motives. If you are doing it for the wrong reasons, you have every reason to wait."

The Fifth Lesson: Say It Now

In everyday life, people often regret things they've said. We lose our temper and let someone have it, only to rue our hasty words. Or we e-mail an off-color joke that comes back to haunt us (and these days, it can travel around the world in a couple of minutes). However, when it comes to deep, long-lasting regret, the experts pointed instead toward things left *unsaid.* The view from later life is this: *if you have something to say to someone, do it before it's too late.* The experts emphasize this lesson either because they are grateful that they spoke up while there was still time or because they profoundly regret not having done so.

Ralph Veliz, seventy-two, reinforced this point by offering an insightful aphorism: "Send flowers to the living. The dead never see them." His rule for regret-free living: *do it now.*

TELL PEOPLE TO SEND flowers to the living. Because by the time they're gone, what's the point in sending them? If you're going to do it, do it now. Don't wait until next week to send those flowers to the living because they might not be living then. If you have a grudge against someone, why not make it right, now? Make it right because there may not be another opportunity, who knows? So do what you can do now.

It is an interesting paradox that people most often regret things left unsaid in their intimate relationships, where we would expect the most communication. The experts realize (sometimes too late) that marriage becomes the domain of the "taken for granted," in which feelings are assumed but not expressed. And that's a source of deep regret for some long-married experts.

Grover Sykes, eighty-nine, loved his wife deeply and several years later continues to mourn her death. He doesn't have many regrets in life, but one stands out:

> COMMUNICATION IS AN IMPORTANT thing in marriage. We probably didn't really express ourselves, either one of us, to the extent we should have. But I think it's very important. Looking back, it could have been better. We had a good but a late marriage. She was the right choice. Oh yes. But I wish we'd worked on communicating. She got a rare disease, and her doctor told her that he could keep her alive for a while with blood transfusions, all kinds of medical care. Or we could take her off and she'd be dead in a month. That's what she decided.
>
> She lasted two weeks. Well, I always regretted it—that we didn't talk more about . . . everything. I wish I'd told her she was the first and only woman that I really ever wanted to marry. I think we were both sort of loath to talk about some things. She was stoic and didn't want to talk about things, and I'm sure I didn't. It's too bad we didn't. You know? I've had a hard time because of it.

Every once in a while an interview moved me to tears. Hal Phipps, eighty-one, was an inspiring respondent, filled with life wisdom expressed carefully and clearly. Hal loved his wife dearly and after fifty-five years of marriage is still grieving her death three years earlier. When asked what mistakes young people should avoid regarding getting and staying married, he responded, "Well, one mistake I made, anyway—and this is hard for me to talk about . . ." He broke off and began to weep. But he insisted that even if it was painful for him, he wanted the lesson he'd learned included in this book.

> THE ONE THING I regret is that I didn't tell her how much I loved her as much as I should have. And I didn't really realize that until I lost her. So I want to tell people to express themselves. She and I both were the kind of people to hold back those kinds of feelings. I don't want to say I took her for granted, but I took those kinds of feelings for granted. I can see in retrospect it would have been much more fulfill-ing for both of us if I hadn't. And I think she probably would feel the same way.

Who knows why it is so hard, even in the closest relationships, to say what needs to be said before it is too late? It may be complacency, people's natural reticence, or the fact that some intimate relationships develop topics that are off-limits to open conversation. In contrast to the regretful individuals, few experts were more grateful than those who had managed to say what needed to be said while there was still time. Often this was the simple phrase "I love you."

In eighty-one-year-old Dennis Setzer's marriage, he told me, "It was very hard to say 'I love you' and that kind of stuff to my wife, Marjorie. And I hate myself for that but somehow it just couldn't come out." A turning point came when Marjorie was hospitalized:

> SHE WAS VERY ILL and when she had her surgery I went into the hospital. I couldn't go the first night afterwards, but my daughter did. And my daughter finally said to me, "Dad, you've got to go see Mom. She's asking where you are." And so I went, and I just broke into tears when I saw her with what they had done to her, you know, and I was just beside myself emotionally. I felt that she came to understand how much I cared, in language and in my behavior, then. That's one of those experiences that make you understand what is and what's not important.

Ruth Helm tragically lost her college-age daughter in a plane crash. As we discussed our adult children, she told me with a smile, "You'll never let go of them, you can't. So it's there—you only want everything good for them, you know? And one thing we always did, whenever we would get off the phone we always said, 'I love you.' And I was so happy that we did that because when I said good-bye to my daughter the last words that I said to her were 'I love you.'"

When you get to be a certain age, almost everyone has something they wish they had said (or asked) before it was too late. I'm only in my midfifties, and I certainly do. For me, it is less what I wish I'd said than what I wish I'd *asked*. Both my mother and my father were only children, so I'm in the unusual position of having no uncles, aunts, or first cousins. There's no one left to inform me about family history. Every so often a question will come up. Something like, why did my father choose to become a biochemist? Or, how exactly did my mother go from being an English and theater major in college to becoming his graduate student? I have a whole list of questions I would give anything for the chance to ask the two of them—but it's too late.

For some regrets, there are possibilities for do-overs and second chances. Unfulfilled goals like not getting more education or not traveling enough, for example, can be remedied until fairly late in life. Leaving critical things unsaid or unasked, however, from begging forgiveness to saying "I love you," can't be changed after the person is gone. Here's where the simplest of actions—a conversation—is a great regret-prevention strategy.

Postscript: Lighten Up

The experience of regret in later life is a painful one, so acting now to avoid it makes sense. And the five lessons in this chapter offer pretty good tips for sensible living, whether or not you are concerned about regrets over the long term. When asked for what advice they would give to younger people, a number of experts suggested, "Stay out of trouble!" These lessons, with their emphasis on honesty, caution in major life decisions, and searching for a sense of purpose, help point us in the direction of staying out of trouble.

Here's the refrigerator list for regret reduction:

1. **Always be honest.** Avoid acts of dishonesty, both big and small. Most people suffer from serious regret later in life if they have been less than "fair and square."

2. **Say yes to opportunities.** When offered a new opportunity or challenge, you are much less likely to regret saying yes and more likely to regret turning it down.

3. **Travel more.** Travel while you can, sacrificing other things if necessary to do so. Most people look back on their travel adventures (big and small) as highlights of their lives and regret not having traveled more.

4. **Choose a mate with extreme care.** The key is not to rush the decision, taking all the time needed to get to know the prospective partner and to determine your compatibility over the long term.

5. **Say it now.** People wind up saying the sad words "it might have been" by failing to express themselves before it's too late. Don't believe the "ghost whisperers"— the only time you can share your deepest feelings is while people are still alive.

This chapter has focused on living a life without regrets. Now that we're at the end, I want to share a secret: "regret-free living" is a bit of an exaggeration. I really do believe that aspiring to a life free of regrets is a worthwhile goal that can help us make better decisions on a daily basis. But there's one more thing the experts know: for most of us, this goal is unrealistic. So they have another lesson for you: *go easy on yourself regarding mistakes and bad choices you have made.* A person with no second thoughts about anything he or she has done is probably someone who hasn't taken many chances in life (something actually worth regretting). The question is whether we let these errors in judgment become regrets.

Alice Rosetto, eighty-five, encourages us to practice self-acceptance as a way of getting over regrets:

WHAT I HAVE LEARNED from the mistakes that I've made is that you can't change what's happened in the past.

You have to accept yourself, warts and all. That was hard for me, because I came out of a background that was telling me if you kept trying harder, you really could do it all right and be perfect. It took me some time to accept the fact that it's not going to work that way. And it's okay that it doesn't work that way, so it's really self-acceptance. Once a decision is made or a direction is started, you don't get anywhere by looking back and second-guessing it. And as somebody taught me years ago: if you've bought a pair of shoes, don't look at the shoes in the next store window.

Marilyn Stiffler, sixty-nine, urges us to treat ourselves more gently and avoid feeling guilty about actions long past.

YOU SHOULD BE KIND to other people, but you also should try to be gentle with yourself. I grew up in a family where there was a lot of worry and a lot of expectations for performance and a lot of guilt. But it's very important as you get older to be gentle with yourself and appreciate who you are, because people are so hard on themselves. Try not to be too judgmental. Take it easy—take it easy on yourself.

The wisest Americans agreed upon this last lesson about regrets: when you get to their age, you eventually need to forgive yourself. If a choice or decision still troubles us after many years, our elders give us permission to lighten up and forgive ourselves. I suggest we take it.

CHAPTER 7

❖ ❖ ❖

Choose Happiness

Lessons for Living like an Expert

Jane Hilliard, 90

MY PARENTS' DIVORCE WHEN I was thirteen was ugly and acrimonious, and my mother, sister, and I suffered severe financial hardship. My school life was important to me and I was disappointed that I was unable to go on to college. World War II affected and changed everyone's life. We truly thought it was to be the war to end all wars. What a bitter lesson that was. I was emotionally and financially unequipped for the grief and difficulties that followed my husband's death in 1952. When I look back now, I wonder how we survived.

But my later years have been much easier because I learned to be grateful for what I have, and no longer bemoan what I don't have or can't do. Saying "thank you" reminds me of my blessings, which are many. When I look back over my life, the most important things I have learned are these.

My small and modest home gives me a feeling of comfort and security.

Being self-reliant and able to care for myself has been part of my mother's heritage to me. She didn't give up when life was difficult and I try not to either. Grief, sorrow, and disappointment are difficult to endure, but in time I realized that there usually was a lesson to be learned and memory has allowed me to remember a person loved who is now gone.

Mother taught me not to cry over "spilt milk." If you make a mess, clean it up. If you break it, fix it. And if you make a mistake, correct it. She also taught me to keep my word, to be dependable, not to rob others of their time by being late, and to promptly return what I borrow. The world would be a better place if we all learned to value each other, to respect each other's privacy and differences, and, most importantly, not be judgmental.

Life isn't fair. I believe it is important to have arms outstretched, holding one hand up to the person who is giving you a lift up, and one hand down, giving someone else a helping hand up. Some days will be passed by putting one foot in front of the other to get through, but others will be filled with joy, every moment worth celebrating.

I have had to live simply but eventually I realized that it is the best way for me to live. To know what is enough, not to use more than my share of the earth's resources, to recognize the difference between wants and needs, to enjoy the pleasure of making something broken of use again, and learning to appreciate simple pleasures has made my life more satisfying and less worrisome. Happiness does not depend on how much we have but is based on personal success of skills and artistry, a sense of humor, the acquisition of knowledge, the refinement of character, the expression of gratitude, the satisfaction of helping others, the pleasure of friends, the comfort of family, and the joy of love.

AS YOU HAVE READ the twenty-five lessons in the previous chapters, it may have struck you that although the specific topics differ the advice has an underlying coherence to it. Like recurring motifs in a symphony, particular themes wind through the experts' recommendations for how we should live our lives. These ways of viewing the world appear and reappear no matter what subject they are discussing. You've probably noticed, for example, how they emphasize time and the importance of spending it well, their deep knowledge of human vulnerability, their sense of the importance of close relationships and open communication, and the role of honesty and integrity that surfaces in many of their narratives.

I've had the benefit of several years of carefully studying the experts' responses to the question, "What are the most important lessons you have learned over the course of your life?" During that time it's become clear to me that their shared experience of momentous historical and personal events, as well as their temporal location at the end of life, creates a general outlook on how to live. There are many individual differences, of course, but after immersing myself in hundreds of interviews, I came away convinced that

America's elders share a worldview that can help us transform our lives. I believe we all can benefit immensely from learning to think like one of the experts.

The five lessons in this chapter tap the worldview that underlies the themes we have heard so far—the conceptual framework that supports the wisdom of America's elders. They encapsulate what I have discovered to be the experts' five basic principles for making the most of your life.

The First Lesson:
Time Is of the Essence

The core of the experts' perspective, what particularly distinguishes their way of thinking from that of the young, has everything to do with *time*. For people in their seventies and beyond, time is truly of the essence; it is the sea in which they swim, and their awareness of time shapes every other lesson they have provided in this book. What older people have that younger people do not is this: the profound existential awareness that each of our lifetimes is limited. The question for the rest of us is, how can we use this knowledge?

It's true that when we are in young adulthood we may get a whiff of the shortness of life—when a college classmate dies unexpectedly, for example. But we generally don't believe in it because the number of years left to us seems so near to endless that there's no need to concern ourselves. In middle age we begin to realize that we are creatures of time, but many forms of denial are available to us, from the second (or third) spouse to faith in dietary supplements to Botox to vigorous workouts in the gym.

But there comes a point in life (and I think of it as somewhere around age seventy) when we truly internalize the idea that we belong to time. We develop what psychologists refer to as a "limited time horizon"—unusually poetic for social scientists, calling up as it does the setting of the sun over the rim of the earth. The experts used a broad palette of expressions and metaphors to share this one fundamental truth: *life is short.*

Sometimes people who have something very important to say, something that they know "deep down in their bones" is true, find it difficult or impossible to get anyone to pay attention. Typically this happens at some point with teenagers. You try to convince them of a fact you know from your life experience—an apparently simple point, such as that studying harder just might lead to better grades. And most of us have encountered the smug look or the rolling eyes that convey, "Yeah, right, but I know better." It's one step away from putting fingers in their ears and singing, "I'm not LISTENING!" With this lesson, the experts are the adults and we're all the teenagers.

From the vantage point of their seventies and beyond, the elders emphasized this particular message with a mix of frustration and urgency. For some experts, this revelation came suddenly; for others, it slowly crept up on them. But nearly all found the speed with which life passes to be breathtaking when viewed from the end—and the oldest were the most surprised. Looking at how younger people squander time, they are like members of a desert tribe staring in dismay at our profligate use of water.

Jordan Chen, sixty-eight, told me:

WELL, I'VE LEARNED THAT when they tell you that life is short, that's what they mean, and it is true. Sixty-eight years have gone by very, very fast, and it seems like yesterday I graduated from high school and that was fifty years ago. And I think probably a lot of people aren't prepared for the fact that life on this earth is but a nanosecond and that's really true.

And ninety-nine-year-old Essie Feist confirmed it:

IT'S JUST—THE TIME goes so fast. I can't believe it. The
older I get, the quicker the time goes. Before you know, I'm
a hundred.

The elders tell us that one day we will stand where they are,
and we too will say, "It is amazing how quickly time passes!" They
want us to acknowledge this unavoidable fact *now*—not to depress
us but to help us to make smarter choices about how we spend our
time. It's not a new idea; indeed wisdom traditions have made this
point for millennia. The psalmist stated it clearly: "So teach us to
number our days, that we may apply our hearts unto wisdom." The
experts know how easily this fact of life is forgotten or repressed.
They suggest we do this kind of "numbering" now, so that we will
make the wisest choices about how to spend our very limited time
and how to make the best use of each day.

The problem for younger people is in the "mechanics" of acting on this awareness. If it is true that we will be keenly aware of
the shortness of life when we reach the end, what should we do?
When a friend dies at a young age, I have grown accustomed to
people's comments about how this makes them want to "stop and
smell the roses," take things more slowly, and so on. However,
within a few days they seem to have returned to their normally
hectic lifestyles, with no apparent change. Jo Barnoe, ninety-four,
points out how difficult it is for the young to keep their limited
time span in mind:

STARTING OUT, THE YEARS just roll slowly. There's no
such thing as looking ahead thinking, "Oh, when I get to
be sixty or seventy." But you're going to get there—we're all
getting there. No one is going to be left out. Everybody is

going to know what it's like to get to be ninety. And believe me it came so quickly I couldn't understand. It came so quickly I didn't know it was happening.

Based on their knowledge of our limited time horizon—that no matter how long you live, life is short—the experts prescribe a specific approach to life for people of any age. And they believe that younger people can put this way of living into practice immediately in their own lives. The moral of the story that life is short is this: take advantage of every day you are given. This phrasing is intentional, in that many of the elders suggested that each day be taken as a gift and treated that way.

A Latin aphorism has come into common usage: "carpe diem." Made famous by the movie *Dead Poets Society*, it is usually translated as "seize the day." The meaning of the original Latin, however, is closer to "harvesting" the day. It is in this sense that the experts endorse carpe diem: that each day has an unharvested abundance of pleasure, enjoyment, love, and beauty that many younger people miss. A very common human failing, they argue, is not taking advantage of life's pleasures and attending to the very joy of being alive. Indeed a number of the experts (Jews and non-Jews alike) quoted a phrase from the Talmud: "We will be held accountable for all the permitted pleasures we failed to enjoy." Many elders personally discovered the importance of seizing the present moment, and it changed their lives.

Genevieve Portas, age seventy-two, told me:

I'M LEARNING TO LIVE in the moment. I feel like you're responsible for what happens in your life. But that can make you think, "I can't wait until . . ." And I've tried to banish that phrase from my life. I spent many years of my life saying, "I can't wait until I have a baby." Well, I passed over a whole part of my life being focused on what was going to happen, which ultimately might not have happened. And I find that when I let things go, they tend to turn out in a more delightful way than if I had tried to control them.

Some of the experts passionately delivered this life lesson because they regretted their own failure to act on the principle that life is short. Fortunately, most learned the "seize the day" mentality in time to change their approach to life. But they nevertheless feel regretful for not having discovered earlier the need to take advantage of every day we are given.

I particularly treasured this letter sent to me by Bessie Sherman, eighty-six, who wrote it to her beloved granddaughter (and we can hope she took it to heart):

> My darling girl,
>
> Don't worry so much. There is not enough time in our lives to trade off the gold of our existence for the dust of what-ifs or what-if-nots.
>
> I had my first job before I was twenty and saved everything I could from my paychecks. I closed my ears to good advice from a dear woman who told me that I should enjoy my days and not become so absorbed with thrift.
>
> I did not understand what she said. Although I used money to attend plays and concerts, I did so knowing that each ticket for a performance meant less money in my savings account. As I grew older, people I knew and loved died, and I began to see how very precious each moment of each day is. Still, worries without end consumed me. I was swept away by the need to make things right, to gain approval for my actions, and to raise upstanding children.

Finally, I came to realize that the intimate connection with those we love is what truly graces our
lives.

Some of the experts learned the importance of attending to
the present moment through loss. Mary Beth Grieshaber, age
seventy-four, told me: "Our son was hurt very badly when he was
four and that may have colored my view that 'life is a gift.' It's a
library book that could be recalled anytime. Not that you don't
want to have long-term plans, but don't put everything off." And
at age eighty-four, Trudy Jefferson's health problems taught her
to "Never imagine that there will be time later to accomplish
something, because that later time will turn out to have been
yesterday."

Most often, however—and despite having learned this lesson
the hard way—there was a kind of joyous exuberance in the experts' responses. One could almost hear a sigh of relief and "Finally, I've got this straight!" in their words and tone. The experts
urge you to be more lavish in how you use your time, to embrace
life enthusiastically. They know that each day is one you will never
get back, so why not make the most of it? Valerie Jenkins, seventy-
four, exemplifies this enthusiasm:

MY ADVICE IS NOT putting off too long to do something,
because there certainly are things to do at certain times in
your life that you can't do at others. There are no wheelchair
ramps to the bottom of the Grand Canyon, so if you want
to get down there, you have to go when you've still got two
little feet.

My favorite piece of advice on this topic came from Harriet
Wagner, seventy-five: skip the funerals and see your friends *now*.

HERE'S WHAT WE'VE TOLD most of our close friends: We're not going to show up at their funerals because we can't stand funerals. But we *are* going to show up at any party or happy thing they invite us to. We'll receive an invitation and because it's in Kansas or South Carolina or some weird place, they don't really expect us to show up. But we do because we love a party. We tell them: "We're not going to come to your funeral, so we're here now." And they love it. They think we're nuts, which we probably are, but we do it. And some of our friends have begun to do the same thing.

If we fail to "number our days," we risk waiting for things to happen instead of making them happen, and living for future events that may turn out to be very different from what we had planned. The experts tell us to strive for happiness with what we are given, right now, and to make this perspective a daily habit. This attitude is the gift we receive from awareness that life is short.

The Second Lesson:
Happiness Is a Choice, Not a Condition

Gretchen Phelps reminded me of a grandmother in a baked-goods commercial, with rounded features and white hair in a bun. Only well into our interview did I learn that this contented and still active eighty-nine-year-old grew up in poverty, weathered the loss of her husband and one of her children, and today occasionally experiences disabling bouts of pain from arthritis. Gretchen nevertheless had a peaceful, strong serenity about her, combined with considerable wit.

When asked about her most important lesson for younger

people, she didn't hesitate: "In my eighty-nine years, I've learned that happiness is a *choice*—not a condition." And it felt to me like a "eureka!" moment.

I pressed Gretchen to describe this idea for me. She explained that taking charge of one's own happiness simply *must* happen at some point if one is going to live a fulfilling life. Not, she emphasized, trying to assume control over everything that happens to us—she laughed at that idea—but over our own conscious attitude toward happiness. "My single best piece of advice is to take responsibility for your own happiness throughout your life."

This lesson turned out to be ubiquitous among the experts. Gloria Vasquez, eighty-six, typifies their experience of this core insight:

> THE BIGGEST LIGHTBULB OVER my head came to me when I saw I could move away from painful situations by using my choices. I didn't have to stay and take the pain. I could initiate change. This was a turning point in my life.

Mo Aziz, seventy-five, expanded on this idea:

> YOU ARE NOT RESPONSIBLE for all the things that happen to you, but you are completely in control of your attitude and your reactions to them. If you feel annoyance, fear, or disappointment, these feelings are caused by you and must be dug out like a weed. Study where they came from, accept them, and then let them go. If you let outside pressures determine how you feel and what you do, you have just abdicated your job as CEO of your own life.

Happiness in the experts' view is not a passive condition dependent on external events, nor is it the result of our personalities—just being born a happy person. Instead happiness requires a conscious shift in outlook in which one chooses—daily—optimism over pessimism, hope over disillusionment, and openness to pleasure and new experiences over boredom and list-lessness. Happiness is created through intentional attitude change—the opposite of the sense of powerlessness inherent in waiting for life to deal out a better hand. Indeed for many of the experts, this point was the first lesson they provided and the core of their worldview.

As you can imagine, many people in this age group have ex-perienced the negative events younger people worry about. It's highly reassuring to know that they feel happiness, contentment, and that even joy can be found in spite of life's problems. The com-bined wisdom of our elders tells us to "roll with the punches," adapting to difficulties as they occur and never losing a sense of the joy that inheres in living in spite of problems.

Marguerite Renaud, eighty, put it this way:

LOTS OF UNPLEASANT THINGS are going to happen to you in life, and when they do you have two choices. You can mope and sulk and feel sorry for yourself, or you can put on a brave face and get on with your life. Sometimes it takes a lot of self-pity before you can get going with the rest of your life, but the sooner you can manage it, the more you will discover that life is worth living after all.

Thus the experts portrayed happiness as an either-or decision. When events occur, they insist, we are not "made happy" or "made unhappy." Instead we can exercise choice regarding how they affect us. Kristy Galvin, eighty-four, argues that happiness doesn't "just come at you," but rather that embracing joy needs to be a conscious personal policy:

LEARN HOW TO BREATHE and move on. There is plenty of pain to go around, but if you get stuck in it, you don't move on. I think you have to adopt a policy of being joyful. I don't think that joy and happiness just come at you. You make them. It's an "attitude of gratitude" somehow. It makes it possible to move through this stuff and come out more or less better on the other side.

After listening to the experts, I came to call their attitude "happy in spite of." This viewpoint contrasts with that of many people, which I'd call "happy if only." The dominant perspective among the young says: "I will be happy if only I . . ." You can fill in the blank as well as I can: if I lose weight, find a mate, get divorced and find a different mate, get healthy, get rich, and on and on. The experts believe that such a "happy if only" attitude is futile and will inevitably lead to disappointment.

Looking back, I recall that this lesson was first taught to me by my younger daughter, Sarah, when she was six years old. A doll was on the market with a feature designed to make it irresistible to a girl of that age: it had long, flowing hair on which she could create patterns with a special set of stamps. I, as a middle-aged man, was mystified as to why someone would spend nights of sleepless anticipation over being able to make blue hearts on a doll's pink hair. But for my daughter this doll was the key to happiness. Well, the big day came, and I will never forget the disappointed look in her eyes after the first ten minutes of play, when she turned to me and wondered, "Is this it?"

Psychological researchers tell us that changes in our circumstances—getting that great job, the move to the Sunbelt you've dreamed about, even getting married or winning the lottery—only give us a temporary "bump" in our happiness level. Generally, after a surprisingly brief period of time, people go back to whatever their original level of happiness was. So for the all if-onlys we set our sights on, there is at best a short-term boost in our happiness level. It doesn't last. Studies show that changes in circumstances have little potential for producing long-term changes in happiness.

Rather than this "happy if only" viewpoint, which is so prevalent among younger people, the experts have a radically different idea. They insist not only that we can choose to be happy but that we can choose to do so on a daily basis *in spite of* the problems that confront us or the lack of something we feel is very important to us. They believe that individuals can change and influence their own attitudes in spite of external stresses and even tragedy. And they argue that it is a tremendous mistake to wait for external events to "make" you happy. This "happiness in spite of" perspective of the elders provides us with some of most hopeful news possible about making the most of life. Namely, that the choice to be happy can—indeed *must*—occur in the face of life's most daunting difficulties.

There are almost as many examples of turning points where people consciously chose happiness as there are experts, and some can point to a specific moment where that decision was made. I'd like to share with you the experience of Ruth Helm, whose wonderful story about finding her true love began chapter 2. Ruth's experience as a Jewish child in Nazi Germany was challenging in a way few Americans can imagine today. Her life changed from a warm family environment filled with school, activities, and parties to one where, "All of a sudden it was the swastika and the uniforms—I was so scared of the uniforms. It was terrifying, because you heard what's going on." Her family fled to the United States and Ruth flourished in America. But not even the events of her youth prepared her for the greatest tragedy of her life.

WELL, NOW COMES THE sad story. I had three children. My youngest daughter, Sherry, wanted to become an actress. She was always performing. Her acting teacher called her Bubbles, because that's how she was—she was a real bubbly girl. So when she was twenty-one she came home one day and said, "Daddy, it's vacation. Can I please go on a trip to the Caribbean? My friend has a friend there. I can stay with her. It'll only cost the airfare." And why would we say no? She was a good girl and she was entitled to go, and so we let her go.

But unfortunately the flight crashed at the airport and she was killed. Twenty-one years old, just a beautiful, beautiful girl. We had traveled so much—it had never occurred to me, a plane crash. You read that in the paper about somebody that you don't know, but not you. Well, thirty-eight people got killed.

Ruth's experience is the worst nightmare I, as the father of two daughters, can conceive of. Without thinking, and probably more intensely than I realized, I asked her, "How can people get over that? Can you tell me what you did?" She nodded.

NOW, I'M GOING TO tell you, this is the story. This was the absolute worst. I wouldn't wish it for my worst enemy. I just lost myself for two years, and that nearly destroyed my family. I became just mechanical. I did everything, but as soon as I was done I went to sleep. Sleeping was my escape. My husband would come home, we would have dinner, I'd clean up, and I'd disappear into bed. Years later my neighbor next door said, "You know, Ruth, you ran away, you went to sleep. Joe came in to us because he needed to talk to somebody." So I did that for two years.

And one day my daughter, Jill, came home from college and she said to me, "Mom, you're always so sad. It makes me feel that I need to run away from you." That was my lesson. Those words turned me around, and I said, "Okay, Ruth, you cannot do that anymore because you're chasing away your other child whom you love, and you're killing your husband." It happened that day when my daughter said those words to me. "Mom, you're always so sad."

That's when I turned myself around. People here where I live think, "Oh, that lady never had a bad day in her life." They always say, "You're the happiest person—you're always smiling and laughing." They should know my background, all the way from what I went through as a little girl to losing a child. That's the worst that can happen to anybody.

But I changed everything. I chose to be happy. And I chose it for my family. I made up my mind—I don't want to hurt my family anymore. And it was hurting them. I was hurting my kids and I was hurting my husband. I told myself that's all I can think of now. I had to preserve them. I had to take care of them. I didn't have Sherry to take care of. I needed to take care of the ones who are here. That's what really pulled me out of it, I'm telling you. So thank God my husband and I still had all those years. That was in the 1970s when she got killed, so we had all those good years before he died.

So maybe you can tell people this story—that you know this lady who went through a terrible time—and you can tell them that she realized that sitting and worrying doesn't get you anywhere. It's just a matter of using your brain that'll get you somewhere. Now you won't see sad in me. You see a smiling happy person.

The question of course arises, How, precisely, do they do this? The advice that we should "choose to be happy" probably makes sense to many people. But most of us could use some guidance in how to *act* on that advice. The consensus of the experts is that the choice to be happy is one that is not made once and for all. Instead it must be enacted consciously each and every day—regardless of external circumstances. The happiest elders feel *empowered*; they have learned to *act*—to move intentionally toward a positive perspective.

When I think of someone who makes this choice each and every day, I think of Mary Farmer. I visited her apartment in a housing complex for older and disabled people in New York City. Mary, sixty-seven, greeted me warmly at her door and invited me to sit down. I immediately took in the extent of her physical impairments. She wears a heavy leg brace and her left hand hangs limply. Her eyes do not focus on me because she has been totally blind for three decades.

In the early 1980s, Mary's life was going well. She described herself as enjoying everything at that age, "I liked to go out and have a good time!" She had a secure job with excellent benefits. Her daughter was nearing her high school graduation, and Mary anticipated newfound freedom. Then, with no warning, she was felled by a massive stroke, transforming her from a hardworking young mother in love with life into a severely disabled woman, dependent on others for her care.

Mary told me:

IN ADDITION TO THE paralysis, my retinas were destroyed. I like to say, "I'm on the front seat for a miracle!" I had to learn a whole new lifestyle. I had to learn to live in a blind world. I lost my independence overnight. I spent a total of eighteen months in the hospital for rehabilitation. Then I came home. I made some progress, but you can see how I am now. I can't see at all, and on my left side I have some paralysis. I also have carpal tunnel syndrome in my right hand—my good hand—and that bothers me, especially at night. I don't get around by myself. I lost my sense of direction with the eyesight. I can't find the way to the end of my block, so I need help every time I leave the apartment.

If I were to stop the story here, you might make an assumption about how it ends. A severely disabled woman grows old, becoming one of New York City's tens of thousands of social isolates, sometimes attracting notice only when they die and their absence is finally noticed by neighbors. But in fact Mary Farmer's life did not turn out that way. She discovered a path through the disaster to what is now a remarkably rich and fulfilling life. She participates in church and volunteer activities, maintains a very active social network, and acts as a peer counselor to other older people dealing with vision problems.

Mary recalls that after her stroke and hospitalization, she reached a decision point.

THE FIRST THING I had to do was decide not to feel sorry for myself. If I hadn't done that, I'd be sitting around having pity parties. You know what happens in a pity party? Satan brings the chips! I realized that I was just so glad to be alive. There was a time when I couldn't get out of bed by myself. That's why I get up so early now, around 5:00 a.m., because I'm so happy I can get up on my own!

You have to do what you have to do. Because that's the way I was raised. Don't drag your behind. Get up and do what you have to do. Do it. Get it out of the way. My mom used to say, "Get up, you can't get nothing done lying in the bed!" That's what I did. I eventually got up and made a life.

As I was leaving, Mary called me back to sum up her decision to choose happiness in spite of enormous adversity:

> JUST BE GLAD THAT you have your life. I'm very satisfied with my life. I mean, I wish I could walk on my own, without the brace. I wish I could use my left hand. But I want every day that I've got coming to me. Every day that the good Lord has assigned to me, I want it!

Like Mary, many experts found that reminding themselves of the gift of life daily helped them choose happiness. Shirley Garry, seventy-three, has had her share of health issues, including heart problems that require a pacemaker, kidney disease, and severe back pain. Nevertheless, she emphasizes at the start of each day that she has a choice about her own happiness. "Each morning, when I wake up, I just say, 'Thank you for this day. This is wonderful. What will I do with it?' Because it's a great life. It really is." She went on:

> BUT IF I SEE I'm beginning to feel bad, then I consciously start counting my blessings. And it sounds silly and simple but it works. It doesn't pay to dwell on how much something hurts. If you pay attention to how much you have got going for you, that makes a great deal of difference. But basically what I have to do is will myself to think about all the great stuff that's going in my life, and there's a lot of it. I've come to be very much at peace with myself, and it's nice.

Antoinette Watkins suffered through the death of her daughter from cancer at age forty-six. Nevertheless, she maintains a very positive approach to life.

I THINK MY LIFE is full of gifts. For example, like my daughter who died. The last two or three years of her life were such a gift to her, and they were a gift to us, and so life itself, the living of life, can be wonderful, it really can. You have to look at it that way too. Good Lord, enjoy it! The most difficult and stressful experience I've had was my daughter's death, and what that taught us is that the loss of a child and a friend will always bring you tears, but the joy of having known them lasts forever.

It's a fact that life will hand us problems and difficulties—if that hasn't happened to you yet, you're lucky (and probably very young). Despite this fact, we all have the power to choose. We can make a conscious decision each day to embrace a positive attitude. It requires convincing yourself that you can wake up and decide to focus on positive emotions. Lest you think I am painting too rosy a portrait of our elders, it is important to keep in mind that *everyone* who reaches their seventies and beyond has experienced tragedy of one kind or another. This is indeed one of the fundamental sources of elder wisdom and a reason why we need to attend so closely to what they tell us—no other group in society has this much experiential knowledge. They have become experts in walking a balance between accepting loss and maintaining an awareness of life's pleasures. The elders overwhelmingly believe that each of us can choose to be happier and that we can do so in the face of the painful events that inevitably accompany the process of living.

The Third Lesson:
Time Spent Worrying Is Time Wasted

Sometimes the experts' message was unambiguous, and so it was with this lesson. When asked what they would recommend to younger people looking for ways to make the most of their lives, many focused on one action: stop worrying.

Over and over, as they reflected on their lives, I heard versions of "I would have spent less time worrying" and "I regret that I worried so much about everything." Indeed, from the vantage point of late life, if offered a "do-over," many experts would like to have all the time back they spent fretting anxiously over the future. As I reflected on my own experience, I realized that this dictum shouldn't have come as a surprise.

I recalled one particular moment when the same truth came home to me. I was in my midthirties and life felt like it was at the full. I was finally secure in a good academic job, I was happily married, and I had become the proud father of two beautiful daughters. My research had received enough notice that I had been invited to another university to give a lecture about it. I arrived the day before the event, and I took advantage of the pleasant afternoon to go for a run around the campus. It was one of those archetypal fall days that makes anyone who ever went to college nostalgic—the air was crisp and clear, the leaves were turning, energetic fresh-faced students laughed on their way to classes.

Filled with a sense of well-being, I fell into a reverie as I was jogging along in which I had a vivid image of a conversation between thirty-six-year-old me and my early twenties self. I pondered what I would say, and let the conversation flow in my mind. It's important to note that my younger self was pretty much an anxious wreck, continually worrying about relationships, finances, the direction of my life, and in particular my career prospects. I was in graduate school during one of the worst academic job markets in fifty years, and my fellow students and I obsessed about whether our Ph.D.s would only entitle us to be very well-educated taxi drivers or call-center operators.

As I spoke back to myself over more than a decade, I found I had a single urgent message I would have liked to deliver: *relax and stop worrying*. I wanted to let the twenty-four-year-old Karl know that he was poisoning the present moment with future anxiety and that what he really needed to do was to have a modicum of trust and stop worrying so much. In my fantasy I longed to be able to tell my less-mature self, "See, everything turned out okay! You're wasting this great period in your life by spending so much time worrying about things that may never happen." My memory of this spontaneous insight made the experts' accounts of this lesson ring particularly true.

Their advice on this issue is devastatingly simple and direct: worry is an enormous waste of your precious and limited lifetime. They suggested training oneself to reduce or eliminate worrying as the single most positive step you can make toward greater happiness. The experts conveyed, in urgent terms, that worry is an unnecessary barrier to joy and contentment. And it's not just what they said—it's how they said it.

John Alonzo, eighty-three, was a man of few words, but I quickly learned that what he had to say went straight to the point. A manual laborer, he had battled a lifetime of financial insecurity. But he didn't think twice in giving this advice: "Don't believe that worrying will solve or help anything. It won't. So stop it." That was it. His one life lesson was simply to stop worrying.

Valerie Armstrong, a sixty-nine-year-old former physician who has seen her share of people in serious trouble, expanded on this theme: "Don't worry. There's never an excuse to worry, and it makes it impossible for you to act appropriately." Noting how much we worry about our health, she went on:

> IF YOU HAVE TO go to the doctor and you're afraid he may tell you something bad, why worry? You don't know that he's going to do that, so you have nothing to worry about and all you do is waste energy. Once he does tell you, there's still no need to worry because now you can do something about it. Worry saps your energy and accomplishes nothing. If the doctor says you have to have an operation and there is a risk involved (and of course there is), gather your facts, discuss it, make a decision, and again you have no need to worry. You've made the decision. What will be, will be.

And James Huang, eighty-seven, put it this way:

> WHY? I ASK MYSELF. What possible difference did it make that I kept my mind on every little thing that might go wrong? When I realized that it *made no difference at all*, I experienced a freedom that's hard to describe. My life lesson is this: turn yourself from frittering away the day worrying about what comes next and let everything else that you love and enjoy move in.

What's important is not just the advice to stop worrying but also how strongly and definitively the experts worded it. They used terms like "there's never an excuse for worry" and "don't." Alice Rosetto looked back on a rich and interesting life and provided a detailed rationale for her rejection of worry. Married for sixty years to a ninety-two-year-old husband who still goes to work every day, and mother of four children, she had a long career helping people with drug and alcohol addictions.

Alice sees worry as a futile attempt to control the fundamentally uncontrollable.

> FOR ME, PERSONALLY, ONE of the important lessons I've learned over the years is that you cannot control what might happen and you cannot change what did happen. I've really come to be able to negotiate life pretty much worry-free. I have learned that if I can't do anything about a situation, then worrying isn't going to change it either.

I'm such a worrier that I struggled to get my mind around this. The idea of not worrying about things is for me like trying to imagine what it would be like to be a caveman or a hobbit. I therefore wanted to know, "Just what does that feel like, anyway, this not worrying thing?" Alice said: "It brings a lot of peace and serenity. This is not to say that I don't get concerned about something. Here's an example. Not too long ago one of my daughters was ill in the hospital, and I was of course concerned for her, but I also realized I couldn't change it. Well, to me worry is the kind of thing that keeps people up at night and that doesn't happen to me, because I know that I can't change it. I have learned just not to do the worry thing."

I found this lesson from the experts to be surprising. Given that they had lived through difficult historical periods and great personal tragedies, I thought they might *endorse* a certain level of worry. It seemed reasonable that people who had experienced the Great Depression would want to encourage financial worries, who fought or lost relatives in World War II would suggest we worry about international issues, and who currently deal with illness would want us to worry about our health.

The reverse is the case, however. The experts see worry as a crippling feature of our daily existence and suggest that we do everything in our power to change it. Most important, they view worrying as *a waste of time*. Recall that they see time as our most precious resource. Worrying about events that may not occur or that are out of our control is viewed by them as an inexcusable waste of our precious and limited lifetime.

How should we use this lesson, so that we don't wind up at the end of our lives longing to get back the time we wasted worrying? I believe that the message itself can influence us on a day-to-day basis, and we should keep it in mind each time we find ourselves worrying unnecessarily. I have found that reminding myself of the experts' recommendation helps me to put worries aside (indeed I use this insight a bit like a mantra these days).

Since most of us could use more help than that, the experts fortunately provide us with some concrete ways of thinking about worry and moving beyond it as we go through our daily life. I think you'll find these specific tips as useful as I have.

Tip 1: Focus on the short term rather than the long term.

I couldn't help it. I tried to treat every interviewee equally, but when you're talking to someone over one hundred years old, it's hard not to give what she says a little extra weight. Eleanor Madison is a delightful, positive 102-year-old who has had much to worry about in her long life. Her advice is to avoid the long view when you are consumed with worry and to focus instead on the day at hand. She told me:

> WELL, I THINK THAT if you worry, and you worry a lot, you have to stop and think to yourself, "This too will pass." You just can't go on worrying all the time because it destroys you and life, really. But there's all the times when you think of worrying and you can't help it—then just make

yourself stop and think: it doesn't do you any good. You have to put it out of your mind as much as you can at the time. You just have to take one day at a time. It's a good idea to plan ahead if possible, but you can't always do that because things don't always happen the way you were hoping they would happen. So the most important thing is one day at a time.

Tip 2: Instead of worrying, prepare.

Lucy Rowan struggled with shyness and social anxiety as a young woman. Now, at eighty, she has overcome her tendency to worry unnecessarily. She found the antidote to worry in careful preparation for situations that make her anxious. Her advice:

> MY MOTHER WAS KIND of a worrier, and I have it too. It comes with the territory, I guess. But I have learned to prepare, to prepare for everything I worry about. Whenever I give a speech or anything, I write it out. I sometimes play the piano in my church, and I practice until I can play it perfectly. It takes the worry away. It's the same with surgery I have that's coming up. I prepared for all the things about it—I've talked to everybody about everything. I'm thinking I'm all set, you know? I'm in God's hands and I've got wonderful people that know their job. And I'm not going to worry, not going to waste time. If you want to maintain good health, spend your time planning instead.

This advice is echoed by many of the experts. They see a distinct difference between worry and conscious, rational planning that greatly reduces worry. It's the free-floating worry, after one has done everything one can about a problem, which seems so wasteful to them. Joshua Bateman, seventy-three, summed up the consensus view: "If you're going to be afraid of something, you really ought to know what it is. At least understand why. Identify it. 'I'm afraid of X.' And sometimes you might have good reason. That's a legitimate concern. And you can plan for it instead of worrying about it."

Tip 3: Acceptance is an antidote to worry.

The experts have been through the entire process many times: worrying about an event, having the event occur, and experiencing the aftermath. Based on this experience, they recommend an attitude of acceptance as a solution to the problem of worry. However, we tend to see acceptance as purely passive, not something we can actively foster. In addition to focusing on the day at hand and being prepared as cures for worry, many of the elders also recommend actively working toward acceptance. Indeed this was most often the message of the oldest experts.

Sometimes the implications of an interviewee's age took me off guard. So it was when Sister Clare Moran mentioned in passing that her grandfather had fought in the Civil War. The Civil War! Part of my surprise came from the fact that Sister Clare looks at least twenty years younger than she is: she will turn one hundred this year. Living happily in her order's residence for retired nuns, Sister Clare remains active and engaged in the community's activities. Before I began this project, I never would have believed what I will tell you now: if you want to hear about an interesting life, sit down for a while with a hundred-year-old nun.

Reflecting on her nearly eighty years in the religious life, Sister Clare pointed to doing away with worry as her lesson for younger people. Early in her career as a nun, she learned a technique for reducing worry through pursuing acceptance:

THERE WAS A PRIEST that said mass for us, a youngish priest, very fragile and frail. Beautiful, beautiful man. He said that at a certain time of his life, something happened. He didn't tell us what it was. I heard that he had been working on a mission and they asked him to come back to the States and it broke his heart. It must have been a very hard thing to do. And he was very angry—he just couldn't be resigned, just couldn't. He got back into work here, but he couldn't get his mind off it. Just couldn't see why it had happened.

So he went to an elderly priest and he talked to him about it. He said, "What shall I do? I can't get rid of it." And the priest said, "Every time it comes to your mind, say this." And the priest said very slowly, "Just let it be, let it be." And this young man was saying it just the way the priest said it, and he said, "I tried that and at first it didn't make any difference, but I kept on. After a while, when I pushed it aside, let it be, it went away. Maybe not entirely, but it was the answer."

Sister Clare, one of the most serene people I have ever met, has used this technique for well over three-quarters of a century.

SO MANY THINGS COME to your mind. Now, for instance, somebody might hurt your feelings. You're going to get back at him or her—well, just *let it be*. Push it away. So I started doing that. I found it the most wonderful thing because everybody has uncharitable thoughts, you can't help it. Some people get on your nerves and that will be there until you die. But when they start and I find myself thinking, "Well, now, she shouldn't do that. I should tell her that . . ." *Let it be.* Often, before I say anything, I think, "If I did that, then what?" And *let it be*. Oh, so many times I felt grateful that I did nothing. That lesson has helped me an awful lot.

A very different woman, a very different life, but a very similar message: Hannah Wrobel was born in Poland in 1912. Her brother had emigrated to the United States and encouraged her to join him. Hannah followed his advice in 1932, but she was the only family member who did so. She told me quietly: "The rest of my family was all murdered by the Nazis. They tried to get out, but it was too late. They couldn't make it. The Nazis took care of them." She paused for a moment and made it clear that she would like to change the topic: "Just how long can you think, how much can you think about this? You can't think too much."

Hannah now lives in a comfortable apartment in Manhattan, helped to maintain her independence by a devoted daughter and an aide who assists her. She lived what she considers a marvelous life in the United States, working on Wall Street for years and married to a successful physician. Perhaps it is this mix of tragic and joyful life experiences that produces her almost unearthly serenity. Hannah could have lived a life of regret, but instead has this advice:

LEARN THAT LIFE IS good. You have to learn from the problems or the problems overcome you. I've learned a lot about life and nothing bothers me anymore. And it gets to be so, and it's just the way it is. Acceptance, yes. If you don't accept it, you go down the drain. Be calm, go with the flow. People worry about dying, about everything. I'm not worried at all. As you see, I'm a very easygoing person. And I take life as it is. If I'm going to die tomorrow, then I'll die tomorrow. How else can you live? Life is short, you have to be open-minded. Very open-minded. Learn to accept instead of worrying—then you will be okay.

Worry is endemic to the experience of most modern-day human beings, so much so that following this lesson may seem impossible to some readers. But what the experts tell us is consistent with research findings. The key characteristic of worry, according to scientists who study it, is that it takes place in the absence of actual stressors; that is, we worry when there is actually nothing concrete to worry about. This kind of worry—ruminating about possible bad things that may happen to us or our loved ones—is entirely different from concrete problem solving. When we worry, we are dwelling on possible threats to ourselves rather than simply using our cognitive resources to figure a way out of a difficult situation.

A critically important strategy for regret reduction, according to the experts, is increasing the time spent on concrete problem solving and drastically eliminating time spent worrying. One activity enhances life, whereas the other is deeply regretted as a waste of precious time.

The Fourth Lesson:
Think Small

When people seek happiness, they often think about big-ticket items: buying a house, finding a partner, having a child, getting a new job, making more money. By now we have seen that from the viewpoint of America's elders, this attitude is a mistake. The lure of being happy if only something in the future happens is, in their experience, a trap, and one that some of them realized only when their lives were nearly spent. It makes sense, then, to ask: What concretely can we do to avoid this pitfall? What's the alternative to either dwelling on problems and deficiencies in our daily lives or orienting ourselves so much toward the future that we ignore the present?

According to the experts, the solution to this problem is to heighten our enjoyment of daily life, even as we wait for our lives to change. Many of them used the image of "savoring" life's pleasures, moment by moment, as one would a delicious meal. Younger people, from the elders' vantage point, are oriented toward major achievements as they seek happiness. They are often obsessed with future plans and involved in such a hectic lifestyle that they cannot attend to the joyful aspects of the present moment.

Because of their limited time horizon, the experts have become attuned to the minute pleasures that younger people often are only aware of if they have been deprived of them: a morning cup of coffee, a warm bed on a winter night, a brightly colored bird feeding on the lawn, an unexpected letter from a friend, even a favorite song on the radio (all pleasures mentioned in my interviews). Paying special attention to these "microlevel" events forms a fabric of happiness that lifts them up on a daily basis. They believe the same can be true for younger people as well.

For many, this was a lesson learned during the Great Depression. That experience of deprivation taught them the intense enjoyment of small pleasures. Our needs and desires have become bloated to the extent that it takes an enormous amount to please contemporary Americans. But many of the experts grew up learning the lesson "savor the small stuff." One of my favorite descriptions of learning to appreciate small, daily pleasures came from Larry Handley:

LET ME TELL YOU, in the 1930s we had the Depression. If you think you got a depression today, it's nothing like it was then. People didn't even have enough to eat back then. A lot of the dads in the neighborhood weren't working. And we shared simple things because people didn't have money. We'd maybe get a nickel once in a while. We were half a block from a wonderful park. They had lots of activities there for kids, and we had a huge skating pond down there. They'd have band concerts in the summer and the whole neighborhood would go down there.

There would be popcorn wagons parked all around in the park. We kids would have a nickel and we'd stand there for several minutes trying to decide, "What should I have?" And these poor guys, they're trying to wait on you. They're patiently waiting for you to decide: "Do I want popcorn or do I want ice cream or maybe a Holloway sucker?" And once in a while, at the movies, they would have Saturday matinees for kids for ten cents. And after the movie, if we had another nickel, we'd stop at a place that had ice cream and popcorn and we'd get that. And boy! We really had a Saturday afternoon.

"And boy! We really had a Saturday afternoon." I had difficulty getting that phrase out of my mind. I have watched children come back from a shopping spree at the mall or a movie at the megaplex, revved up on candy at ten dollars a box, and I don't think I ever heard one of them sigh contentedly, "Boy! We really had a Saturday afternoon."

So one thing that clearly distinguishes the experts' approach to happiness has to do with what some of them termed the relationship between "big things and small things." Ursula Lauterbach, seventy-six, brought this point home to me. Her life has been one of much upheaval and significant tragedy. Raised in the former East Germany, she was a child under the Nazi dictatorship, cowered in bomb shelters during the war, and experienced the deprivation of the postwar years. What a lifetime of experiences like this produces, Ursula told me, is the ability to *think small*:

I THINK THE MOST important thing I learned was not to take things for granted. You cannot be entirely prepared for what will happen to you in life, but I learned that despite everything that happened life is worth living and you can enjoy every day, especially because of the little things in life. You can have joy even if the big things go wrong.

Lydia McKeon, seventy-three, adopted this viewpoint later in life, after spending much time as a younger person worrying about the future. Her advice:

ENJOY LIFE. ENJOY THE little things. However small they are, they're still enjoyable, but a lot of folks don't see that. I look at things differently in that I don't get as stressed out about things. Now that I'm older, I see my children in their circumstances and they get stressed out over things and I realize that I don't think about those things anymore. I know now that these problems will pass along and come out the way they will. I just sit and enjoy folks. I just enjoy talking to them or taking a long walk. I let the dust build up. I don't worry about the dust anymore. Used to. Don't anymore.

We might think that this sort of savoring is fine as long as you're feeling well and otherwise enjoying life. I learned, however, that the reverse is more typically the case. The presence of illness or disability actually enhanced the interest in, and ability to savor, daily pleasures. For many of the experts, appreciation of small "bonuses" in life was bound up with the experience of health problems. Tamara Reed, seventy-two, experienced this firsthand:

I HAVE BEEN VERY ill, so unfortunately I've spent most of my time recently dealing with those illnesses. The past year has been particularly difficult that way. I needed brain surgery and then I had a heart infection, which required antibiotics on a daily basis, and I was in a nursing home for a while. I learned that you must adapt and enjoy what you can. If you look, there are always things you can enjoy. You can see the beauty of a flower. You can hear beautiful music. As long as you have faculties that allow you to see and hear, you can adjust and appreciate that life is worthwhile.

Marianne Rumsey, seventy-six, has suffered from a discouraging number of health problems in recent years. She sees the sense of fragility that belongs to these experiences as directly contributing to her ability to savor:

WITH PHYSICAL PROBLEMS YOU have gone through, the day-to-day becomes more important because you don't know what tomorrow is. That became much clearer to me after I'd had my two or three heart episodes. Enjoy each day, if you feel fine today. There are no guarantees for the future. It sounds trite, but it's so true, really is and we all forget about it, but it's important to remember. Lighten up, let's look at things and be happy instead of being glum and negative. Walk cheerfully on the face of the earth.

Okay, so we should savor the minute pleasures of life and let the big things we can't control take care of themselves. It's good general advice, but I wondered if there were more concrete ways people like me could put this insight into practice. I'm not by nature a "savor the present moment" kind of guy. In fact, I tend to focus on what's going to happen next. I can be out for a run on a beautiful day, but I'm mostly thinking about the hot shower and cold beer afterwards. And then, when that's happening, I will be thinking about work tomorrow. And when I'm at work—well, you know how it goes. The experts exhort us to make savoring a conscious act, to treat pleasures in the current moment as special gifts. It's a shift in consciousness that we can reinforce daily with a little effort.

Flora Turnbull, who enlightened me about many facets of elder wisdom, is a poet and what I would call a philosopher of everyday life. At age eighty, she continues to publish poems that express her love of the landscapes of the Southwest. Her approach to living is to embrace the pleasures each day holds, and she reinforces that attitude with a daily habit:

> I LIKE TO START out the day with a list of ten things that I'd like to do that day. Now, I'm not going to accomplish all of them and probably only one of them is going to work out, but I never know which one, at the beginning of the day. It's not a "to do" list—it's just a list of what I would like to try doing. I'm always looking for new things to try. They don't have to be difficult things—I'm probably not going to take up hang gliding or something like that. Something simple. Finding new opportunities and new challenges each day.
>
> If I were to give any particular word of advice, I would say, go about the business of the day, humdrum as it might be, but walk on your tiptoes, waiting for the "aha!" experiences. That happens when you're going around the corner doing the normal, everyday things. So be prepared for those "aha!" experiences that may happen anytime. That way you're always open to, and watching for, something different—watching for a feather from an angel's wing.

Cynthia Visser, eighty-four, highlights the conscious, planned focus on small pleasures in the "now":

> MY LESSON HAS BEEN looking for the things that I find are delightful. Just looking out my window is delightful, so

it's not that I have to be running around all the time, you know? Watching the deer or the silly dog—not going on vacation, but just standing there looking at things like this. So I take a lot of pleasure in lots of small things each day. For example, on the days I do my taxes I make a point of sitting down and looking at my pictures of the parks I have visited. Physically, I'll sit down and pull out Yosemite or Yellowstone or something. We have to find these small, delightful things.

A number of the elders tied the idea of savoring the moment to feelings of gratitude for the small gifts life offers. Indeed savoring and gratitude go hand in hand: both require viewing even routine pleasurable daily experience as a gift. Renata Moratz has long pondered the mysteries of aging and at seventy-seven leads groups of older people in discussing their roles as "sages." She encapsulates the "attitude of gratitude," treating each day as precious and savoring daily pleasures, no matter how small. She told me:

WHAT'S DIFFERENT ABOUT AGING is that you don't have fifty more years when you're seventy. That's the difference—limited time. And the main thing that results from that knowledge is gratitude. The grateful knowledge that today is another day. Every day I say, "Yes, I'm alive." And every night I say, "Thank you." I always pick the most simple, most mundane thing to be thankful for, because that's where it's at.

June Kim, seventy, is a former philosophy professor and a social activist. She learned the lesson of gratitude during her own bout with cancer and from her husband's heart problems.

MY LESSON CAME FROM my kids. Each of them gave me a word that has been crucial in my life. One of my children gave me a keychain with "trust" on it and another one gave me a stone that had the word "rejoice" carved in it. Those two things run through my life. Trust and be grateful and rejoice. Be grateful for all the beauty and everything you see and do.

There is a final component of this lesson: the experts want you to use this perspective now, and not wait until your life is almost over. Malcolm Campbell, seventy, spent much of his career as a workaholic college professor, driven to succeed at a prestigious Ivy League university. Health problems and the breakup of his marriage in his sixties led him to rethink his approach to life. He learned savoring and wants younger people to start the process earlier than he did:

IT SEEMS TO TAKE a lifetime to learn how to live in the moment but it shouldn't. I certainly feel that in my own life I have been too future oriented. It's a natural inclination—of course you think about the future, and I'm not suggesting that that's bad. But boy is there a lot to be gained from just being able to be in the moment and able to appreciate what's going on around you right now, this very second. I've more recently gotten better at this and appreciate it. It brings peace. It helps you find your place. It's calming in a world that is not very peaceful. But I wish I could have learned this in my thirties instead of my sixties—it would have given me decades more to enjoy life in this world. That would be my lesson for younger people.

I find this lesson from the experts to be especially compelling, and it's led me to make small but persistent advances in my own ability to savor the small joys of daily life. Take nothing for granted, our elders tell us, because you can never be sure of the future. Experience a sense of gratefulness for the fact of being alive and for the innumerable simple pleasures that are available in any given day or hour. Most of us will almost certainly develop this ability late in life; a question to ask ourselves is why not create a savoring approach to life in one's twenties or thirties rather than in one's eighties or nineties?

The Fifth Lesson:
Have Faith

Understanding how to "think like an expert" would not be complete without bringing up the topic of religion and spiritual life. "The sea of faith," as the poet Matthew Arnold called it, is wide and deep among America's elders. Over and over, interviewees told me that a fulfilling life without faith of some kind is for them a contradiction in terms. For many, faith is like a second nature; even describing why it is so important is difficult because it is so close to the core of their belief system—indeed to the core of their very being.

Before going any further, however, let me offer a minority report. There are perfectly happy experts for whom religious faith has no importance whatsoever. Some were raised in religious households and communities but found that religion lost meaning for them. People like Barney Ruloff, ninety, who considers himself a realist. "I'm not a religious person," he explains. "I don't believe in life after death and this heaven and hell and so on. It's philosophically possible, scientifically improvable, and to me it doesn't matter. I just try to live a good, honest life." Others grew up without religion and stayed that way. When asked his religion, Mark

Lightman, sixty-nine, replied: "Militant atheist. In terms of religion, I don't buy it."

But although the experts weren't unanimous, those who did not see faith as a core component of their well-being were relatively few (I would estimate that no more than about fifty of the thousand respondents declared definitively that they had no use for religion or spirituality whatsoever). There is no question that for a happy and meaningful life America's elders almost universally endorse the lesson: have faith.

This message came from Christians, Jews, Hindus, Buddhists, and Muslims. Interestingly, even individuals who scoffed at organized religion or who declared themselves outside of the religious mainstream were among those who recommended some kind of transcendental faith to members of younger generations. Many experts offer this lesson, not to recruit or convert you, but because they believe *it works*. Belief in God and engaging in religious practice are seen as a path to greater happiness in life.

Why do so many older Americans suggest developing the spiritual dimension of life when they are asked for the most important lessons they have learned? Let's set aside for the moment the question of whether religion is actually *true*. I have my own beliefs about this and I'm sure you do too, so I'll leave it at "I won't show you mine if you won't show me yours." It's way beyond the scope of this book to take on the question of whether the entity all those people are worshipping really exists—your priest, minister, rabbi, imam, guru, or other spiritual advisor is the one to answer that one.

But leaving the theological implications aside, the experts recommend spiritual belief and practice because they believe *it is good for you*. They hold that there are major benefits to involvement in religion of some kind. Except in a few cases, the lesson the elders provided wasn't "believe in Jesus and you will be saved" or "convert to Islam." Instead the experts said things along the lines of Maria

Perez, seventy-nine: "Well, I feel like people should pursue some type of spiritual endeavor, and their life will be a lot easier if they follow the teachings of whatever manifestation they choose." Sol Worthington, eighty-seven, shared this view: "I believe younger people should have a faith, they should understand what life is about, who they are, how they fit into the universe, and figure out a creed to live by."

The lesson was typically worded as an endorsement of spirituality itself, however the individual decides to put it into practice. They point to two main reasons why practicing a faith is an important lesson for living: it provides a source of community, and it offers unique help with coping in times of trouble.

For some experts, a personal spirituality is all they feel they need. Jillian Pebley, eighty-eight, told me, "I may not be religious, but I am still a very spiritual human being." However, the majority of the experts argue that we miss some benefits of the spiritual life if we don't practice it with others. They make clear that there is something special about regular participation in a religious group that is highly beneficial. If you have no interest in religious participation and you know you never will, go ahead and skip this part of the lesson. But if you are one of the vast majority of people who does have some belief in a higher power (regardless of how amorphous), then think seriously about the experts' recommendations that you become involved instead of sitting on the sidelines.

In fact, research suggests that church participation provides benefits that cannot be found elsewhere (or at least not easily). No matter what the religion or denomination, people who actually attend services tend to be happier. Studies also show that religious attendance is strongly related to self-reported happiness and that being "engaged" in a congregation leads to greater life satisfaction. Further, people whose religious participation is more frequent show greater ability to cope with life crises.

Interestingly, for some of the experts religious life means participation in the life of a church without a deep personal spiritual experience. Maureen Stewart, eighty-one, has attended church all her life. When asked about the role of religion and spirituality for her, she said:

> I BELONG TO A church here, and we are there every Sunday. I have been very involved. I'm church elder and I chair the mission committee. So religion is a big part of my life. I wouldn't say I'm very spiritual though. I don't know what it means to be spiritual. I'm too practical to be spiritual, maybe. There are a lot of theological things I have a great deal of trouble figuring out. Don't know as I ever will. It's the community feeling, the activities, that I appreciate.

Chris Schultz, eighty-three, has a similar perspective. He was raised a Lutheran in the upper Midwest, and his description of his small-town (population: two hundred) upbringing sounds a lot like Garrison Keillor's Lake Wobegon. He too emphasizes the church community rather than subjective spiritual experience.

> I'M VERY ACTIVE IN a local church. We try to go every Sunday. But I'm not a particularly strong believer in the stuff that's associated with what churches say they're about, the afterlife kinds of questions, that sort of thing. There is one thing, though, that is important to me and the reason I participate. That is the sense of community that can come from people who also are concerned about the world. For people who don't take part in that church community, I think their lives are less rich. I grant that you can get it from other sources, but the church has some unique characteristics about it.

As we grow older, religious congregations provide an extraordinary source of "latent" social support that can be quickly and effectively activated in times of crisis or illness. Kate de Jong told us in chapter 6 about the heartbreaking struggles in her marriage. For Kate, her church has been a crucial source of social support: "The church community means a great deal to me. Some of my best friends are there. So it's like family. In some respects it's even more than my own blood family." This community has supported her through her personal problems:

> AT ONE POINT I got to what I felt was at the bottom of the fringe on the bottom of the rope I could hang on to. But I also had a really strong faith journey through all of it. That's what has kept me going and made me aware that there's value even in unpleasant experiences. It isn't something I wanted. It isn't something I expected. But it has certainly strengthened my faith tremendously. And when I came to the realization that I didn't have to carry the load alone, it made all the difference in the world.

If I had any doubts about the value of a spiritual community for the experts, it disappeared on a cold November day when I sat eating dal (lentils) and roti (bread) in a cultural center in Queens, New York, that serves older Hindus. Many of the center members emigrated from Guyana and other Caribbean countries, which I learned have large populations of Indian origin. In addition to the standard senior center activities (recreation, educational programs, health screenings), the elders come to the center for yoga, meditation, chanting, and dance. Center members provide spiritual support to one another, visiting the bereaved and carrying out the Hindu custom of singing at funerals.

I am always skeptical when people say they can "feel the energy" in a room. But there's no other way to describe the atmosphere of the center, where multiple activities take place in one large hall. All around me, very old but amazingly spry center members chatted, sang, and did yoga. When I say "spry," I mean that they engaged in yoga postures that would have left me partially disabled. I met more friendly and engaging people than I could keep track of, who were introduced, according to local custom, as "Uncle" or "Auntie."

I spent time with Auntie Deepa, a wiry, energetic eighty-year-old with a ready, warm smile and a lilting Guyanese accent. In answer to my question about the secret for a happy life, she referred without hesitation to her spiritual beliefs:

> WE SHOULD LIVE A life where we pray and we can help people. Give prayer for everything. That's what I believe in—that's part of the blessing. You do not have to go to church to get the blessing. You have to pray anywhere you are—our religion tells us that. Anywhere, you keep on singing your prayers. You keep on giving thanks for everything, God is part of everything, everything we do. We buy a new car and come home—we have to pray over the car. We say God bless us all, God bless this city, God bless America, and God bless the whole world.

But the Hindu center itself was also of tremendous importance to her sense of community and connectedness:

> I LOVE THIS CENTER! We come here and we sing good songs and we sing songs to dance to. We listen to nice music and we dance because we're happy. The people here in the center are very happy. And every Monday, Wednesday, and Friday we do a little walk. Everybody from the center goes

for a little walk, to stay healthy. Oh, I am telling you, I enjoy a lot of the people that come here! We call each other brother and sister, that's how close we are. And some tell you their own worries, and you tell them yours, and you get a little consolation, you give a little advice. It is wonderful, if you have a place like this.

So a major component of the experts' lesson about the value of faith is to *actively participate in a religious community.* This kind of religious involvement provides a connection to others that is difficult to find elsewhere in our culture. Furthermore, churches are among the few age-integrated institutions in American society. A number of my oldest interviewees reported that the younger members of the parish came to take on supportive roles that are usually played by family members.

Many of the experts also recommend faith as a way to cope with the inevitable pain and loss that come with a long life. Faith places suffering in context and allows them to accept disability, illness, and the death of loved ones without losing heart. Indeed some of my interviewees expressed being mystified at how others without faith weather life's tribulations. For some deeply religious individuals, it is their faith in the healing power of God and in the afterlife that has helped them through difficult times. For less traditionally religious elders as well, spiritual beliefs allowed them to make the most of their lives despite hardship.

I met with Curtis and Barbara McAllister over coffee in their comfortable kitchen. Curtis, seventy-four, and Barbara, seventy-three, are a strikingly fit, attractive couple—indeed they met me fresh from a morning workout at the gym. But appearances can be deceiving: Barbara and Curtis have coped with much more than their share of health problems. In his thirties Curtis had life-threatening encephalitis. Barbara told me, "He'd call me from work and say, 'You'll have to come get me today because I don't think I can drive. My arms aren't working.' He got better—we were lucky because some people never recover."

Even more serious was Barbara's long-term struggle with cancer, which runs in her family. Barbara was in her late forties when she was diagnosed with stage 3 ovarian cancer. "It was really bad. I had chemo and surgery and I was out for a year. But I got better, which was surprising. I didn't think I was going to make it but I did." A recurrence eleven years later was also successfully treated.

At that time Curtis and Barbara decided to retire and enjoy each other, their children, and their grandchildren. But the disease was waiting to haunt them one more time. In his early seventies, Curtis was also diagnosed with cancer; he's now in remission. This couple wanted me to know that they were by no means "religious fanatics." But they strongly recommend the support of religious faith for getting through the kinds of life crises they have experienced.

Barbara, having lived through life-threatening illnesses and painful treatments, told me:

ABSOLUTELY, OUR FAITH HAS been huge. That's the big part of it—our faith and our beliefs. I truly feel that God is always with me. I feel that even if something happened at the end, we're never alone. God is with you, or the divine presence or whatever anyone wants to call it. It doesn't matter as long as you have that belief. And that makes a huge difference. Because when it's too tough for you to handle, you just say, "Okay, it's up to you." To God or whatever. "Okay, I've done what I can and it's up to you."

Curtis echoed this perspective.

I REMEMBER WHEN BARBARA started getting crazy symptoms in her abdomen and not too long after that she had ovarian cancer. And then she had a recurrence a few years ago. I mean, she's like a living miracle. We prayed—we gave thanks to God. Maybe he did cure her, but it's more just the fact that we were in his care, no matter what. Whether she actually died or got better, we had faith in God. Not in a religious-fanatic way or anything like that. She did a lot of meditating and all kinds of things that help people cope, relying on God to help her. There's a lot more to life than just existing on your own. I think we all need some spirituality, having faith that there's more to life than these years, these seventy-five years. And that there are rewards after this.

For less traditionally religious experts, participation in ritual still helps them cope with life's tragedies. April Stern told me:

WE'RE JEWISH, AND RELIGION was very important to my husband. As years went by, it became more important. It has not been a very important part of my life, and I don't believe in God. But I have to say that there are certain rituals that have been important to me. At the time of my husband's death, I found that the Jewish mourning rituals were very comforting. And I enjoy holidays now because of the family spirit of them. I feel a sense of Jewish identity that has little to do with religion, but more a sense of connection to a community.

There's one more thing to say about the experts' views on religion, and in this day and age it's very important. It probably has come as no surprise to you that spirituality and religion play a major role in the lives of America's elders and that they recommend it to others. But I hadn't expected how much they would also endorse tolerance of others' beliefs. The vast majority of the experts argued in favor of religion as one pathway to making the most of your life. But very few had any interest in telling you exactly what religion you should practice. This was true for many deeply religious experts. Renata Moratz typified the experts' viewpoint, combining as she did her own firmly held religious beliefs with tolerance for other paths:

> THERE IS A REALITY that is one of the roots of my essence. I have no memory of a time when I did not know that I was loved by God, a generous, omnipotent divinity. This reality led me to the liberating message of the Gospel of Jesus, the Christ. But it doesn't matter what church you belong to or don't belong to. If Muslims were here, Hindus were here, Buddhists were here, Jewish people were here, they would all tell you that their religion says, "Love one another and forgive one another." That's the common thing.
>
> I was leading a group, and one man said, "All you have to do is believe in Jesus Christ as your Lord and savior. That's all you need." And I said, "Oh, you are so blessed to understand that and so I'm happy for you, but everybody doesn't believe that and everyone's beliefs are different."

Or as ninety-seven-year-old Cora Jenkins put it: "Have a deep but unfanatical faith in a higher being. It is basic to a caring, generous, whole human being who can maintain equilibrium in a turbulent world." "Deep but unfanatical" is a perfect characterization of the elders' recommendation about developing a healthy and fulfilling spiritual life.

Postscript:
The Golden Rule

In this chapter America's elders told us about the big picture. What can we do to lead the happiest life possible? They bring to this question long experience of life's challenges and difficulties, firsthand knowledge of major historical upheavals, and their unique point of view, looking back from the last part of life. It's a big task, but the experts were up to it.

Here's the refrigerator list:

1. **Time is of the essence.** Live as though life is short—because it is. The point is not to be depressed by this knowledge but to act on it, making sure to do important things *now*.

2. **Happiness is a choice, not a condition.** Happiness isn't a condition that occurs when circumstances are perfect or nearly so. Sooner or later you need to make a deliberate choice to be happy in spite of challenges and difficulties.

3. **Time spent worrying is time wasted.** Stop worrying. Or at least cut down. It's a colossal waste of your precious lifetime.

4. **Think small.** When it comes to making the most of your life, think small. Attune yourself to simple daily pleasures and learn to savor them now.

5. **Have faith.** A faith life promotes well-being, and being part of a religious community offers unique support during life crises. But how and what you worship is up to you.

I want to leave you with a final piece of the experts' wisdom in which all five of these lessons are intertwined. To be honest, it's one that took me a while to figure out. There are certain expressions that have great weight for the experts and that fit especially well with their way of looking at life. We've seen examples in earlier chapters, like "don't go to bed angry." These maxims seem to have deep meaning, so much that the elders were sometimes at a loss to describe precisely why they are so important. It's like the old English-class exercise of writing an essay on how to tie your shoe: you know it so well that it's hard to put into words.

One of these sayings, however, outshone the all rest. It came up again and again in answer to various questions, including, "What are the most important lessons you have learned over the course of your life" and "What are the major values and principles you live by?" In fact it was probably mentioned more often than any other single piece of advice. What was this important truth? It first came to my attention when one of our eager young research assistants, who was helping us code the lessons, came to me and said, "Dr. Pillemer, I was just wondering—do people really care this much about the Golden Rule?"

The Golden Rule. Many of you will remember it from Sunday-school classes. When describing their core values, some elders just said those three words:

> **Interviewer:** What are the major values or principles you live by?
> **Expert:** The Golden Rule.

Often they would paraphrase it, offering versions like "Do to others what you want them to do to you," or "Treat people the way you want to be treated." Some answers were even more free-form, such as "Do unto others as I wish they'd do unto me," or "Do unto others and you pay for what you do that is against people," and the negative version, "Don't do unto others what you don't want done unto you." Very frequently they stopped with the signature three words: "You know, do unto others . . ."

Why? I asked myself. Why the Golden Rule? I don't have any comparison data, but I sincerely doubt that people my age and younger would give the Golden Rule as their guiding principle. Drilling down was a challenge, because many experts found it unnecessary to explain why the Golden Rule was the way to live. So I decided get some help about what the Golden Rule actually means. Fortunately scholars have looked at just this question. Jeffrey Wattles's book, titled—surprise!—*The Golden Rule* was the most definitive I could find.

The version of the Golden Rule that most of the experts learned in Sunday school comes from the King James Version of the Bible and goes like this: "All things whatsoever ye would that men should do unto you, do ye even so to them." But one reason why the Golden Rule comes up so frequently is that every religious tradition has a version of it. Hinduism: "Knowing how painful it is to himself, a person should never do to others what he dislikes when done to him by others." Judaism: "What is hateful to you, do not do to your neighbor." And Islam: "None of you truly believes until he wishes for his brother what he wishes for himself." Still, I had trouble understanding precisely how it figured so centrally for America's elders.

Obsessed with this issue, I went back and read everything the experts had said about the Golden Rule. And I slowly came to understand what kind of guidance for good living they are proposing. Their reliance on the Golden Rule is at heart an emphasis on compassion. This word perfectly sums up what they were telling me; its literal meaning from the Latin is "suffering with." "Do unto others as you would have them do unto you" means that we must work hard to empathize with other people, to understand their perspectives, to feel as they feel, to see them as fellow travelers along life's difficult road. Such compassion and empathy makes it natural to treat others as we would like to be treated.

For many experts, the pivotal importance of fellowship with other human beings was learned through a panoply of challenging, tragic, and uplifting experiences. They often put it simply: "Be kind to others," or "Be a friend and lend a helping hand," or "Treat others with respect."

Mabel Leutz, ninety-one, summed up this life lesson with the word "love." Like other experts, she has come to feel grateful for the opportunity to act with love and compassion, and to regret times when she failed to do so:

> I GUESS THE MAIN thing is love. Give love, let your kids and grandkids know you love them and their families. If I could do anything differently in my life, I would be more compassionate about people in general. You know, you're very critical of certain people, but now that I realize what they went through I would be much more compassionate. I would recognize their good points and I wouldn't be so critical. I have come to appreciate their lives more and more.

I will give the last word to Joshua Bateman, whose recent illnesses have brought the meaning of life into focus for him. He told me that when it comes down to it, making the most of life means connecting to and caring about others:

> WELL, WHO HAVE YOU helped? What circles do you move in? Who likes you? Some people I've known, they never helped anybody. They never did anything. They were never in any circles—they lived their own life totally unto

themselves. You know what? Nobody would go to their funerals. It would be as though they never passed by on earth. They didn't make any ripples. They didn't interact or help or do anything to build up anyone else. And on the positive side, I got to know a great old lady and there were over a thousand people at her funeral. So if I stick my head in a hole and think of just myself, and I don't try to do some good and get out and interact and use my brains to help people, then nobody will come to my funeral. And I'll deserve it.

CHAPTER 8

The Last Lesson

THE ELDERS TELL US that everything comes to an end sooner or later. As you have reached the end of this book, I've reached the end of a project that has consumed me for more than five years (one-sixteenth of my expected life span, if you are counting). I can echo the experts' sense of how quickly time passes: where did five years go? And where is the person who embarked on this project with the barest sense of what he was looking for? At the start I had an urgent but ill-defined desire to know what America's elders could tell me about living the good life, before they were all gone. This quest changed me, as I hope reading this book may have changed the way you think about making the most of your life.

Over the years of working on this project, I had the unique and extraordinary experience of entering people's lives for a brief period (an hour or two) and asking them fundamental and deeply existential questions. What are the most important lessons you have learned for living? What are the major values or principles you live by? Do you think much about dying and how do you feel about it? What advice would you give younger people about marriage, work, child rearing, health, and the spiritual life? Miraculously, over a thousand older Americans took up the challenge and opened their minds and hearts to me.

Sometimes I laughed with them, when they told me things like:

> I WAS POOR, SHY, and backward until I graduated from college. I married a gal who educated me on the finer things in life (don't pick your nose in public, change your underwear daily, take regular baths, and brush your teeth). My advice: marry someone who will diplomatically take you in hand and educate you.

> MY LESSON? STAY OUT of trouble—and steer clear of other people's wives.

> DON'T WEAR A MINISKIRT when you're sixty-eight!

Sometimes they cried, and I cried listening to them, when a story like this was quietly shared:

> WELL, MY DAUGHTER DIED a few years ago. I think about her. I go back over in my mind when she was five,

when she was ten, the things we did. What it would be like if she was here now. You don't forget them. You communicate with them in your head a little bit and remember them.

I live in a big old Victorian house and I have one of those wraparound porches. In the summer when it's nice I'll sit out there and I'll just let my mind float where it wants to go. Sometimes I think of her, you know? And I think of little funny things that happened and I'll laugh, and if anybody went by they'd think, "Boy, she's gone around the bend." But you do that, you know? And after a while you learn to live without her. You get up in the morning and you go through your day, and pretty soon you get up in the morning and you go through more and more and more days without her. So that's how you do it.

As this project comes to an end, I realize how much I will miss the excitement of getting to know one more person, hearing a lesson I'd never thought of, receiving a particular insight that told me something new about the elders' view of life. I will miss the moments of surprise, like having an elegant and cultured woman in her nineties offer this recommendation for sexual fulfillment in later life: "Find yourself a younger man and pay for him!" (Yes, that really happened.) Or the septuagenarian who asked if I minded if he "smoked some pot" during our interview. (Couldn't use that one.) I will miss my interviews with couples married fifty years or more, witnessing the comfortable love (and sometimes the passion) that never went cold. And I know I will miss the "time machine" feel of sitting with people who had listened to Civil War veterans reminisce or had cheered the parades celebrating the end of World War I.

I will miss the diversity of the experts. They came from all over: Texas, California, New York, and all the states in between. Some were immigrants seeking better lives or escaping from political turmoil and persecution in their native countries. I came to love their accents, which are stronger and less homogenized than those found among the young. There was the Texas accent with its soft, musical drawl and slow cadence. "Yes" is transformed to "yay-yes," "twenty-five cents" to "twenny-fi cints," and "government" to "gummint." There were rapid, clipped discussions with New Yorkers, dropping their *r*'s and changing *th* to *d* so that I heard a lot about "muddahs" and "faddahs." Then there were my interviews with members of the Hindu community who emigrated from the Caribbean to New York City. That accent mixes the Indian and the Caribbean, a little of the pleasant singsong but with a clipped, faster pace, turning "with" to "wit" and "that" to "dat." I treasured them all.

Most of all, I will miss them—the experts themselves. The average life span in the United States is around seventy-eight years, which is more or less the average age of the people I interviewed. Some of my interviewees have already left this world. (And given that their beliefs about the afterlife differ so greatly, at least a few were in for a surprise!) Ten years from now (just twice the time I spent on the project), fewer than a quarter of the elders in this project will still be alive. That's how precious this resource is and how rapidly it is dwindling. The world will go on—the experts would be the first to assure you of that—but forgive me if I think it will be less interesting without this remarkable generation.

While they are still with us, however, there is one action we can take: *listen to them*. There is no question that such listening benefits our elders. Over and over, the experts expressed excitement and gratitude over being interviewed. One happy interviewee told me: "It is very nice of you to ask my opinion about life, since my wife and children would rather I pontificate elsewhere!" They expressed satisfaction that their wisdom—sometimes gained at great personal cost—might benefit younger people.

But it's really we who have the most to gain by seeking the life wisdom of older people. We can take advantage of years of lived experience, perspectives that defy contemporary "common sense," and experiential knowledge that comes from having been tested in almost unimaginably stressful and difficult situations. It's the practical side of our elders that is invaluable, which is precisely why I chose to call them the "experts." I seek them out frequently now, and it's a source of endless delight. I recently had lunch with a ninety-three-year-old colleague, retired for twenty-five years. He is an eminent scholar with vast administrative experience in higher education. I told him about a number of the issues I am dealing with on the job and, to his surprise, asked his advice. I came away with a sense of history that put my problems in context, and with at least four concrete ideas for changes to be made. It was well worth the cost of a lunch.

To be honest, though, most of the experts were pessimistic about the outcome of this book. It's not that they felt their advice isn't worthwhile—the opposite is true. They are convinced that younger people can benefit from their long and extraordinary life experience, and they deeply wish that they could be seen as mentors and sages—as they would have been in times past. But they have become convinced that they are irrelevant and that their viewpoint will be seen as archaic.

To me this is astonishing. In the current hard economic times, why wouldn't we want to hear advice on how to live well from someone who made do with almost nothing in the Depression? Given the stresses contemporary military families experience, what would keep us from wanting to understand how families coped during World War II? In today's rapidly changing, postmodern world, what could be more useful than the elders' advice on staying married and raising children?

One reason why we don't ask older people for advice and wisdom is because we don't see them much. We've moved away from a time when people lived together in multigenerational households (or stayed in close proximity to their extended families). Today many older people live alone and children tend to be geographically dispersed. More important than what occurs in families, however, is a strange cultural phenomenon in contemporary society: rigid stratification by age. It's a very rare thirty-year-old who invites a seventy-year-old friend over to share a pizza and watch the football game. Studies show that almost all of our friends are within ten years of our own age, and many are within five years. Most people are more likely to have a close friend of another race than one who is twenty years older or younger.

A first step in breaking down the age barriers is to talk with one another. I strongly recommend that you spend some time asking older people in your social network the kinds of questions that were asked of the experts. Following this chapter, you will find a list of questions that I guarantee will make for good conversation. Or you can take this book to elders you care about and ask them if they agree with the lessons here. Was similarity the key for them in marriage? Or are they an exception? What do they feel about child discipline or (if you want to risk a touchy subject) parental favoritism? Do they have regrets like the ones described in chapter 6? Or do they come up with something different? Do they agree that life is shorter than you think, that you can choose to be happy, and that people should just stop worrying? My dream would be to see this discussion taking place around dinner tables across America.

I have seen how well such conversations work. While I was writing this book, my daughter and son-in-law (Hannah and Michael) took my list of questions to Michael's beloved Aunt Jo, age ninety-four. They spent an hour going through the questions and hanging on her every word, learning about her childhood, her late husband, her work as a dressmaker to celebrities, and her views about love, loss, and the meaning of life. Michael had known her for thirty-five years—but never exactly in this way, through the lens of her lessons for living. It was an extraordinarily meaningful experience for them. It's one thing to ask older people for their stories, but it can be deeper and more rewarding to ask them their advice for living.

Every human lifetime has a beginning and an end. But although the individual human being is lost, the legacy doesn't have to be. We are fortunate that lives overlap in a way that ties even long-past historical periods to the present day. At one point I had a stunning realization. My 102-year-old interviewee was born in 1908. Her grandfather was born around 1850 and told her from personal experience about the Civil War and its aftermath. Take one more step back, and when her grandfather was a young child, the oldest person he knew would have shared firsthand memories of the Revolutionary War!

This is how knowledge for living was once transferred: the experience of interlocking lives, intertwined over generations, was passed along and remained alive in the telling. This wisdom exists in people you know, right here, right now. And it's yours for the asking.

TEN QUESTIONS
TO ASK THE
EXPERTS IN YOUR LIFE

❖ ❖ ❖

1. What are some of the most important lessons you feel you have learned over the course of your life?

If the person has difficulty getting started, try this follow-up question:

- If a young person asked you, "What have you learned in your _____ years in this world," what would you tell him or her?

2. What kinds of advice would you have about getting and staying married?

Follow-ups:

- What's the secret of a long marriage?

- What mistakes should young people avoid regarding getting and staying married?

- What advice would you have for a younger couple thinking of calling it quits?

3. What kinds of advice do you have about raising children?

Follow-ups:

- What mistakes should people avoid in child rearing?

4. Do you have any advice you can share about finding fulfilling work and how to succeed in a career?

5. Some people say that they have had difficult or stressful experiences but they have learned important lessons from them. Is that true for you? Can you give examples of what you learned?

6. As you look back over your life, do you see any "turning points"; that is, a key event or experience that changed the course of your life or set you on a different track?

Follow-ups:

- What are some of the important choices or decisions you made that you have learned from?

7. What would you say you know now about living a happy and successful life that you didn't know when you were twenty?

8. What would you say are the major values or principles that you live by?

9. Have you learned any lessons regarding staying in good health?

10. What advice would you give to people about growing older?

APPENDIX

How the Study Was Done

THIS BOOK IS BASED on information collected from older people using several different methods. In this appendix I will refer to these data-collection activities as the Legacy Project. There are aspects of the Legacy Project and this book that follow standard methods of sociological research. Throughout my career, I have conducted many such studies and published the results in scientific journals. For this book, however, the ways I interpreted the results and wrote up the findings differ occasionally from the standard social-scientific approach. My goal was intentionally to slip free of some of the confines of my scientific work, engaging in much more interpretation and personal involvement than I do for research articles. I wanted to provide a deeper understanding of the worldview of America's elders and to convey their lessons for living in rich and nuanced detail.

The Legacy Project

The Legacy Project followed a series of steps that characterize research in a new area. When I became interested in studying the practical advice older people might offer younger generations, I first tried to find existing literature on the topic. Although much has been written in scientific journals about wisdom in older people, I was surprised to find that no one had surveyed elders about the concrete lessons they feel they have learned over the course of their lives or their practical advice for younger generations. Thus, it was a good topic for new exploration. The following steps were followed to collect data for the project.

Phase 1: Pilot Studies. When sociologists encounter an under-researched area, we often begin with a pilot study—some kind of initial data collection that shows us the lay of the land. What I first needed to do was to answer the questions: Would older people actually have ideas and opinions about life lessons, and would they be able to articulate such ideas if asked? With the help of my research assistants, I set out to find answers.

We began by contacting alumni of several colleges. We wrote to former students age sixty-five and over, asking them to send written responses to the following question: "What are the most important lessons you feel have learned over the course of your life?" I was surprised and delighted when letters came in from across the country. Some responses went on for pages, in the precise handwriting taught in the early decades of the last century. A number of the oldest respondents dictated their answers to younger family members. We then created and publicized a website nationally. Elders—who are more tech-savvy than we acknowledge—gave us their thoughts via the web. Approximately five hundred written responses were received by these combined efforts.

Using these responses, I developed a set of general categories of potential life lessons and created an open-ended interview protocol. Assisted by Cornell undergraduates, we conducted pilot face-to-face interviews with approximately eighty elders from many walks of life. These interviews allowed the elders to describe their views in more detail and to provide life history information that formed the background to lessons learned.

In all, we received many wonderful, detailed responses. However, as a social scientist I knew one thing was missing. We sociologists depend on "random samples" of the population. That is, we do surveys where everyone has an equal chance of being selected, which allows us to generalize to some degree beyond the actual group of people who are interviewed. Of course individuals who choose to write a letter or visit a website may be a bit different from other older people. So my next step was to do something about this.

Phase 2: National Random-Sample Survey. With the assistance of Cornell's excellent Survey Research Institute, I surveyed a national sample of people age sixty-five and over. Individuals from around the country were selected at random and called on the telephone by trained interviewers. The interview began by asking in general about their most important lessons for living that they wished to pass on to younger generations. We then asked the interviewees what they had learned in specific domains, including work and career, marriage, raising children, health, and religion and spirituality. We also asked if there were any problems or difficulties in their lives that had taught them valuable things, and what core values and principles they lived by. Finally, we asked if they had any advice for younger people about how to age successfully.

How, you might ask, did they react? Of course these days people are a bit suspicious when a telephone interviewer calls them, even if it is from Cornell University. One fellow quipped, "What have I learned from life? Not to answer surveys over the phone!" Most people were intrigued, however. One woman said, "I'm glad you called—I could write a book about that." Some were amazed that anyone would ask. An eighty-year-old man told us, "I was sitting here, just staring out the window, and suddenly the phone rings and you're asking me something as profound as this?"

The national survey conducted interviews with 314 respondents (with an average age of seventy-four), and lasting about twenty minutes each. All of these interviews were tape-recorded and transcribed, and I treated them as narratives, reading and rereading each one. I also did simple coding of the responses in different domains to get a general sense of the kinds of lessons that were viewed as most important. A major advantage of the national data is that it confirmed the findings I was getting from the more selective, "convenience" sampling, allowing some confidence that the patterns of lessons were representative of elders in the general population.

Phase 3: Systematic In-Depth Interviews. After spending months reviewing all of the data so far collected, I decided that a final step was necessary to complete the picture of the practical wisdom of America's elders. I had collected written responses and conducted relatively short personal interviews. I realized that there were still a number of unanswered questions and that I needed to include a more detailed, in-depth method of interviewing. I had also learned two important things from the previous data collection. First, there are many people who have led interesting lives but who are not easily able to relate their experiences to lessons for living. So I wanted a sample of people who were more likely to be able to articulate life lessons. Second, I learned that people were much better at answering the questions if they had some time to think about them in advance. So the last stage of the research included two features: individuals were nominated because of their perceived wisdom, and the interview topics were provided to participants in advance.

I asked professional colleagues and agencies to nominate people over the age of seventy for interviews. Many wonderful interviewees were provided by Brookdale Senior Living, a premier provider of senior communities across the country. Other sources included senior centers, a number of New York counties' Offices for the Aging, the Cornell Cooperative Extension system, the Weill Cornell Medical College, and other groups (see the acknowledgments for details). I also included discussions with personal acquaintances about their life lessons. These nominations resulted in approximately 240 additional respondents (with an average age of eighty-one). I conducted around seventy-five interviews myself, and the rest were conducted by interviewers hired and specially trained for the project. These interviews were considerably longer (typically one to two hours).

Thus, although for convenience I refer to the "thousand elders" in this book, in reality information was obtained from close to twelve hundred individuals. Despite the different sources of information—from a national random sample to a mail survey to in depth interviews—the perspective of the elders was remarkably consistent, resulting in the lessons I have presented in this book.

Analysis. I did not rely on quantitative statistical techniques in analyzing the data. As noted, simple coding was done that informed those few times in the book where I say things like "one of the most frequently mentioned lessons . . ." However, the data analysis followed the widely accepted approach in sociology of qualitative and narrative analysis, in which I read all the interviews, sometimes dozens of times, extracting major themes and the components that made up those themes.

Finally, like all university-based social science studies, this project was reviewed and approved at Cornell for what is called "protection of human subjects." This means that certain procedures had to be followed regarding how the data were collected. It's worth noting that, unlike in many surveys, participants in this project were not promised total confidentiality. They were not identified by name—all names in this book are pseudonyms, most created by a random name generator. But they were informed that I intended to use direct quotes and that it is possible that they could be identified by the details in the quotations. No one refused after being given that warning; indeed some wished they could have had their real names next to their lessons.

How This Book Differs from a Social Science Study

The data collection procedures, then, followed standard social science practice. I balanced purposive samples of individuals who were specifically interested in the topic with a representative national sample of people selected at random. However, this is of course a popular book for a general audience. Therefore some things I've done in presenting the information are different from what I would do if I were publishing the data in a scientific journal.

First, I have edited the quotations in the book to make them more readable, cutting out "ums" and "ahs" and making grammar more standard. I have not indicated missing segments of quotations, and I think readers will be grateful to be spared sentences like "Well, um, I guess . . . my most important lesson, hmm, I'm not sure . . . probably was . . ." However, the quotations used in this book all capture the spirit of the recorded interviews. I have kept the tone and expressiveness intact, so readers can get the full flavor of the life lessons.

Second, in most cases the description of individuals is accurate (for example, where they live, age, number of children). However, in a few cases, because of the sensitive nature of the quotes used, I have changed some descriptive details or created composites to make the individuals less identifiable. Although all participants agreed to have anything they told me used, I wished to avoid having any of them regret that decision, especially if minor details would make them easily identifiable to family and friends.

Third, I have taken another liberty in this book in the interest of readability. The Legacy Project involved around seven hundred interviews, all of which I could not have personally conducted. However, I designed all the questions that were asked, I carefully trained the interviewers, and I met with them for supervision. I ensured that all questions were asked just the way I intended and went over the taped and transcribed interviews countless times. I also conducted many interviews personally. For this reason, I use the first-person pronoun in this book for all the interviews that were conducted. Again, I believe readers will thank me for not repeating "Interviewer 6 asked . . ." and going instead with the clearer "I." I believe this is justified given my intensive involvement in all aspects of the data collection process.

Finally, much more than in a scientific study, I have inserted myself into the interpretation and presentation of the information. This project was in part my own personal quest, and my reactions and experiences appear frequently in the book. Similarly, I made decisions regarding the selection of the lessons based on my own reaction to and interpretation of the elders' responses; as noted earlier, the lessons did not emerge from quantitative analysis, such that some received more "votes" than others. This book is the product of my interaction with the interview material, both as a social scientist and as an aging human being trying to apply the lessons to my own life.

NOTES

CHAPTER 2: Great Together

15. **Surveys in fact show that marriage:** Arland Thornton, William
G. Axinn, and Yu Xie, *Marriage and Cohabitation* (Chicago: University of Chicago Press, 2007).

15. **The noted family historian Stephanie Coontz:** Stephanie
Coontz, *Marriage, a History* (New York: Viking, 2005), 309.

42. **proportion believing that "divorce is always wrong":** Naomi
Gerstel, "Divorce and Stigma," *Social Problems* 34, no. 2 (1987):
172–86.

CHAPTER 3: Glad to Get Up in the Morning

52. **in a given year, around 574 million:** "Expedia.com Survey Reveals Vacation Deprivation Among American Workers Is at an All Time High," Expedia.com. May 23, 2006.

57. **People with hedonic motivations:** Edward L. Deci and Richard M. Ryan, "Hedonia, Eudaimonia, and Well-Being: An Introduction," *Journal of Happiness Studies* 9, no. 1 (2006): 1–11.

CHAPTER 4: Nobody's Perfect

89. **an essay by former treasury secretary Robert Reich:** Robert Reich, "Being a Dad: Rewarding Labor," *USA Weekend*, June 13–15, 1997, 10.

112. **Surveys show that tolerance:** Kaiser Family Foundation, *Inside-OUT: A Report on the Experiences of Lesbians, Gays, and Bisexuals in America and the Public's Views on Issues and Policies Related to Sexual Orientation*, 2000.

CHAPTER 5: Find the Magic

126. **During the George W. Bush era:** Terence Hunt, "Bush Marks Birthday with Calls, Surprises," *Washington Post*, July 6, 2006.

128. **Psychologist Todd D. Nelson:** Todd D. Nelson, ed., *Ageism: Stereotyping and Prejudice against Older Persons* (Cambridge, MA: MIT Press, 2002), ix.

137. **The World Health Organization:** World Health Organization, *Preventing Chronic Diseases: A Vital Investment*, 2006.

141. **There's even a whole school:** Douglas P. Cooper, Jamie L. Goldenberg, and Jamie Arndt, "Examining the Terror Management Health Model: The Interactive Effect of Conscious Death

Thought and Health-Coping Variables on Decisions in Potentially Fatal Health Domains," *Personality and Social Psychology Bulletin.* Published online before print June 2, 2010, doi: 10.1177/0146167210370694.

148. **in their book *Successful Aging*:** John W. Rowe and Robert L. Kahn, *Successful Aging* (New York: Dell, 1999), 153.

CHAPTER 7: Choose Happiness

226. **The key characteristic of worry:** Bart Verkuil, Jos F. Brosschot, Thomas D. Borkovec, and Julian F. Thayer. "Acute Autonomic Effects of Experimental Worry and Cognitive Problem Solving: Why Worry about Worry?" *International Journal of Clinical and Health Psychology* 9, no. 3 (2009): 439–53.

246. **Jeffrey Wattles's book:** Jeffrey Wattles, *The Golden Rule* (Oxford: Oxford University Press, 1996).